UNFOLD YOUR MAT, UNFOLD YOURSELF

UNFOLD YOUR MAT,
UNFOLD YOURSELF

Essays on Yoga's Healing Truths and So Much More

ANNE M. SAMIT

Cover Design by Ariel Kaye

Production Assistance by Kawthar Nakayima

Printed in the United States of America

By Anne M. Samit

ISBN-13: 978-0692289501

ISBN-10: 069228950X

For those who've taught me to move on the mat, and for those who've moved with me.

Contents

Contents

Contents

Contents

Contents

Introduction

Some truths we hold in our minds. Some we hold in our words. And when our thoughts and words are beyond reach, our bodies speak for us.

Yoga moves me in the direction where my mind and body strive to occupy the same space. It's the place where they share the same language and where the words all fit on the same page.

It doesn't take much to make this happen. I lift my arms. I lift my heart. And I lift my gaze.

The practice is how I come out of stillness. I move and I move and I move and, before I know it, I find my voice in the places where before I was silent.

The words pour out to heal what's needed. They're all there, waiting to speak the truth.

Through yoga, I move into my life, and my life starts moving. And then I write it all down because how can I not?

And that's the truth as it's written here.

Truth 1

Transformations can be made
when new perspectives are forged.

Beginning

It was the middle of fall, the days were getting shorter, and darkness was falling earlier and earlier.

This is usually the start of a sort of hibernation for me, driving home from work in the crisp and cold with the evening stars already shining. It's not really the time of year for me to embark on any sort of change.

During this time, I'm not sure what made me finally take action on what had been sitting on the floor of my car, among so many other things. It was an advertisement for a local yoga studio.

I looked at the schedule, chose a class, called a friend and showed up. This was a very big deal for me, never having been a big exerciser and never having joined a gym.

I arrived at the studio equipped with the following inexperience: a few yoga classes with my daughter once upon a time, dance classes at summer camp many moons earlier and, in another lifetime, dancing on my middle and high school dance squads.

The music started, and we all stood at the tops of our mats. The music, *my music* of Paul Simon, Bob Marley, Elton John and more, filled the room as the instructor took us through flows of poses, taking the time to walk around and adjust our positions.

The studio was warm, both the atmosphere and the temperature, the rubber mat seemed to anchor me to the wood floor, and the mirror at the front of the room reflected the class moving at all levels but somehow together.

Something in me connected to the music and the long ago dance lessons, and the flow and instruction had a hypnotizing effect.

I was hooked.

Eager to come back, I peeled myself out of bed the following weekday morning. Still not believing what I was doing, I had a little coffee and drove to the studio.

Crisp and cold with the morning stars now shining, I showed up for class and for what would become the highlight of my days.

And just like every day is a bit different, so is every practice. I have discovered that yoga has the power to change my mood, my outlook, my body, my life. Its impact has been nothing short of marvelous, offering up surprising discoveries and interesting insights at a point in my life where I thought I had it all figured out.

I didn't realize it was a beginning. I didn't know I was starting over and that the learning had only just begun.

'Tis the Season

Five hundred, twenty-five thousand, six hundred minutes. How do you measure a
year in the life?

~SEASONS OF LOVE, RENT

When is it time to start something new?

And when does that something new become part of what you always do?

Most things seem to have a season, and I've always found comfort in the traditions that follow.

Come spring, I'm on the porch and planting flowers outside the front door. Come summer, I'm slowing down and wearing more freckles. Come fall, I'm in my jeans and boots and celebrating Thanksgiving and, come winter, I'm hibernating, popping out only for the holidays.

Like clockwork, the seasons pass, a quarter of each year like a quarter of each hour; the minute hand, like our lives, gliding through whatever it is we do during those times.

Off schedule and out of the ordinary, I started going to yoga during the fall season, right before my usual winter hibernation. And something happened once I started to practice. My seasons seemed to collide. It didn't really matter anymore what was going on outside. I just wanted to be inside, in the studio and on my mat.

I went to yoga in the dark. I went to yoga in the light. I was there in the cold, in the snow, in the ice, in the rain, in the heat, in the sun, in the clouds.

This came as such a complete surprise to me, the fact that all I wanted to do was practice. Yoga brought me into a new season, one that wasn't on my calendar, one that I hadn't planned.

Really, I didn't know and never thought that there'd be a new season for me.

But gradually and persistently, yoga brought me out of some kind of shell. I had been in some kind of enclosure without even knowing it.

Recently, on a chilly spring day, I was running around New York City with my daughter. She is a jewelry designer and her errands often take her to what I call hidden places. In this industry, many offices are reached through locked doors and down narrow hallways to windowless rooms at the top of winding staircases, all several flights above the street. You have to know where you are going and, once inside, you can't even tell what time of year it is outside.

We stepped out of a rickety, old elevator and pressed the doorbell, which at once sang out the tune, *Joy to the World*.

It's Christmas in here, I said to the man who answered.

It doesn't matter the season, he said, as we collected the pieces we had come to pick up.

I liked how it was spring, how there were no windows to see the sun, yet the doorbell invented the holiday season year round.

I figure if it can be Christmas in March, then I can embrace a new season for me, too. I had no idea this could happen midway through my life. The physical practice of yoga has reintroduced me to myself, and I'm still figuring this out. I think it's been the actual *moving* on my mat that has brought me out of so many years of what I now recognize as a lengthy winter. The movement is energizing. My body moves and so many emotions and feelings that had been in many ways sleeping have come awake.

I don't consciously think about this. It's just what has happened. I am just more awake these days, and I don't want to sit around anymore.

My yoga practice has taken me to several studios, and I seem to be all over town, back to the places I frequented many seasons before as a young adult. One studio is near where I lived following college; another is close to our old nighttime hotspots, and one more is located near the neighborhood of my earlier married days.

So maybe yoga has me living my life in reverse, seeing that I am at all of my old haunts. It certainly has brought my body back into the shape it was during those days, and maybe I dare say I'm even stronger.

But reflecting on all this, I have to admit that I don't know what's next. If I'm not going around the clock as I had been, then where am I now headed? Where does this new season fit on the calendar that I long ago organized for myself but which no longer applies?

Once upon a time, I wanted to be a writer. Yoga put that on the schedule, too. For the first time, I am writing and people are reading. The other day I was exclaiming about this to my mother.

I always wanted to write, I said. *I can't believe I'm writing.*

And what was it she said back? Of all the responses she could have had, what she said to me was, *'Tis the season!*

How she knew, I don't know. Maybe she has had several new seasons herself. Maybe we all have.

Coming and Going

It's a beautiful morning ... I think I'll go outside for a while ... Ain't no sense in staying inside ...

~A BEAUTIFUL MORNING, THE RASCALS

Leave your mind and arrive in your body.

These were the words of the yoga instructor that opened the class on a snowy Saturday afternoon.

It was the middle of fall, and the snow was unexpected. For some reason, both snow and rain make me want to step outside and go somewhere. This snow was mixed with a bit of rain which prompted my venture out of the house.

I signed up for a class downtown, put on my yoga clothes, added a layer of jeans and long sleeves and topped it off with a down jacket and rain boots. My first stop was a store on the main street for a pair of fingerless gloves.

Breathe, the instructor says. *Use your breath to be present. Not just in your practice but in your life.*

We set up in Down Dog, and I press my feet and hands into the mat with my hips in the air. I turn the eyes of my elbows toward each other and pull in my belly, my body forming an inverted V alongside those of the others.

For several years after college, this downtown spot was my neighborhood. I shopped here. I worked here. I lived here. These days, if I feel the need to get away, to step out of the usual, this is where I go. Driving into town and parking is like leaving one life and arriving at another.

I park on a side street and walk through the neighborhoods down to the main street. Here I can shop the stores, grab a cup of coffee, watch the people and pick up a yoga class. This is costly yoga, though. One time, it costs a pair of jeans from a nearby boutique; another time, three sweaters. Many times, it costs sushi or sashimi. But today it costs only a pair of fingerless gloves.

A crowd of people is departing the narrow entryway of the yoga studio as I and others arrive. The people leaving look replenished and pleased, and a part of me is a bit jealous that they already have that energized feeling that follows a yoga class. It's that endorphin rush that produces a simultaneous sense of elation and serenity. I can see it on their faces as I step aside to make room for their exits before entering the studio from the cold.

I unpeel my layers, stow my jacket, gloves and boots in one cubby, and peel off my jeans and shirt and place them in another.

Breathe. Let go. The instructor's words help us to arrive.

The yoga is hot with the room heated to 95 degrees, the mats crowding the room with only inches to spare in between. I feel a change just stepping into the studio, having walked through the cold, wet snow while bundled in three layers to now breathing in the heat in my next-to-nothing yoga clothes.

The class starts by chanting three Oms, which always feels a little funny. No one exactly sings out; rather, it's just loud because of all the people.

This particular instructor counts a lot. We go through a series of poses, and he counts backward. *Five, four, three, two and one.* We flow into another pose. And he counts, again. The class breathes and sweats, breathes and sweats.

I can feel my thoughts and my muscles loosen, and I get what he says about leaving the mind and arriving in the body. I look ahead at the windows, now all fogged up and sweating just like us. Ninety minutes pass quickly.

We finish by chanting three more Oms, which now doesn't feel funny at all. In fact, the class now sounds like a choir.

Afterward, I layer up and step back out into the cold. In the last hour and a half, I have left my mind and arrived in my body. Replenished and pleased, the endorphins rush over me, producing that mix of serenity and elation.

The snow has stopped, and the sky is almost dark, and I am ready to go home again.

Perspective

The colors of the rainbow so pretty in the sky ...

~SOMEWHERE OVER THE RAINBOW, ISRAEL "IZ" KAMAKAWIWO'OLE

One summer evening, I was scheduled to pick up my parents from the airport after their two weeks of travel.

I raced to finish a chock-full day to meet their flight home. The rainy rush hour had the traffic wound up tight. I turned on the radio and flipped through the stations and talked on the phone.

I arrived at the airport with time to spare and time to buy a chocolate bar. For me, going to the airport is like going to the movies. I have to buy some candy.

Standing at the arrivals, I looked down at my phone to realize I had a voicemail. It was my mother, letting me know they had missed their connection, and that they would be arriving four hours later at another airport!

Homeward bound, I drove through the rain, finishing my chocolate bar and finally arriving home after what amounted to a two-and-a-half-hour roundtrip.

I was a bit cranky. It had been too serious a day, and I felt wound up like the traffic, still in my suit and heels from 10 hours earlier.

I went into the house, took off my clothes, started a load of wash and climbed into bed. I considered the day done until it was time for another try at pickup later that night.

It was only seven o'clock in the evening. What was I doing in bed?

I realized I might be done with the day, but I wasn't really tired. I was just more frustrated than anything else, that was all.

So I hopped up, put on my yoga gear and got back in the car to drive to an evening class.

The rain had let up. The sun was setting.

Being more of a morning person, I mentally tried to energize myself. At yoga, if something isn't possible in a pose, we're told to energetically imagine making it possible. I pulled up to a red light and tried to energetically wake myself up, taking a deep breath and looking up at the sky.

And there, above me, were the most magnificent rainbows I had ever seen! Four concentric rainbows flowed from my side of the street, up and over to the street on which I was about to turn. To get to yoga, I had to follow the rainbows!

Red, orange, yellow, green, blue, indigo, violet. Four arcs of seven colors up and over my head.

Lovely and amazing. Inspiring and energizing.

I felt myself unwind.

This beautiful sight changed my perspective on the day, and I arrived at yoga ready to go. Somehow, I didn't have to work too hard anymore to undo the day. I had already left it behind at that red light under the rainbows.

You come here to unravel, the instructor told us in one of our final resting poses. *In yoga, you unravel your body and unravel your day.*

The practice left me feeling like the rainbows, lovely and amazing, and I left the studio and went straight to the airport.

The rain had stopped, the roads were clear, and I arrived inspired and energized, with time to spare to welcome my parents home.

Transformation

Hoping for daylight to follow me. If you're lost in the dark
get to where you can see.

~DAYLIGHT THE DOG, O.A.R.

I have lived many lives.

Childhood and adulthood and motherhood. Single life and married life and single life, again. Career girl, stay-at-home mom, and working mom of adult children. Head of a full house and head of an empty nest.

Each transition requires a transformation of sorts, some kind of shake-up that propels me from one life to another. In the moves between lives, I can always look back to see how far I've come from where I've been.

Transformation is big! That is, until I found yoga.

In yoga, I experience small transformations that are impactful all the same. In yoga, I arrive at class in one state of mind and body and leave in another.

I've worked closely with a man who served in the Special Forces as a Green Beret, and in his terminology the wake-up hour for any early morning practice is called *O'Dark 30* – before sunrise. I've often wakened in the dark so I can be on the mat for an early morning yoga class.

In general, mornings are pretty easy for me, but sometimes they can arrive too soon. Some mornings, I find my way back into bed - yoga clothes, coffee and all - not once, but twice, before leaving the house. Other mornings might follow a middle-of-the-night phone call from one of my adult children on the way home from someplace late or just in need of a chat.

The *O'Dark 30* wake-up call does not allow for time beforehand to gather any perspective. There is no day under my belt before arriving at class; instead, there is only time to get up and go, and I arrive in whatever state of mind and body that rolled out of bed with me.

On such mornings, the instructor dims the lights before starting the music.

One particular morning, I trickle in with the other *O'Dark 30s,* lay out my mat and put up my hair. The class sits in unusual quiet. There is no usual morning chatter as we wait for instructions as to how to begin, with me hoping to start on our backs and ease into the practice with various stretches.

But on this day we start in Boat, one of my most dreaded poses. Sitting on the tailbone, the body forms a V with the feet out front at eye level, the torso upright, the belly pulled in, and the arms lifted.

We unfold, flattening out our bodies just inches above the mat, and then we rise into a V once more. Torture! We do this again and again and again, engaging the entire body from head to toe.

Following Boat, we stay on the floor for some stretches and twists, my favorite being the one where we gaze over the shoulder and wind our hands between our legs to form a bind.

During these twists, I like to look out the windows at the top of the back wall. On this day as yet I can't see out. The windows are still blanketed in black, the sun yet to rise.

We move into several flows and sequences, hitting most all of the poses we've been taught. The class moves quickly for me and, by the end, I am completely energized, my mind and body awake for the day.

Before our final resting pose of Savasana, we twist again.

I look back over my shoulder and, this time, the windows behind me are well lit. Night has transformed into day, and the sun is shining just like me.

Unwritten Stories

Today is where your book begins. The rest is still unwritten.

~UNWRITTEN, NATASHA BEDINGFIELD

My son was home for a holiday, and we had the rare occasion to tool around town, having lunch and the chance to walk and shop in the sunshine of the first warm day of the season.

I have no place I have to be, he exclaimed, grateful for such unusual circumstances. *There's nothing I have to be doing right now.*

We stopped in a refurbished firehouse that was home to a cool new shoe store. The interior was designed like an old library and, as we sat down on a plush, oversized couch, I pointed out several shelves of blank books, none of which had covers, words or titles.

Look, I said. *None of the books are written. They're all blank.*

My son was busy talking to the salesman. Turns out, they were close in age and knew some of the same people from a few years back.

So, to answer me, my son was really on another subject.

You know, I find myself feeling nostalgic for when I was a few years younger, he said, while holding a shoe in his hand. *And I know that means I'm going to feel the same way later about this time now.*

I used the years I had on him and those blank books as vantage points, telling him that's how it goes, that the challenge lies in being present, because we can always reminisce about our past stories, even as we anticipate those ahead.

I think we all have a story we tell ourselves. It's how we outline our lives, determining who we've been and where we think we're going. I'm grateful that my son was already figuring out his, there in the shoe store, because it's taken me quite some time to do so for myself.

For some reason, it's taken the practice of yoga to unfold my story.

For a long time, I kept my story from most others and even from myself. In fact, for a long time, I couldn't even find the words for it. It was like one of those blank books high on a shelf, and having it out of reach like that allowed me to sit in a sort of stillness for quite a while.

And then came yoga, and I started to move.

It was weird at first, and I was pretty self-conscious. Practicing took a lot of encouragement and a lot of perseverance before it settled into my bones and became a part of me.

Over time, it was as if each pose lifted a piece of my story off the shelf and brought it to eye level, demanding a read, a critique, a review.

Now I'm more of an open book, almost the opposite of me. And I'm writing. A little here and a little there, I'm letting myself be known. I write about yoga and before I know it, I'm writing about myself.

And it's in this way that I'm discovering my story, my take on who I was and how I got to be where I am, even if I'm not always so sure of where I'm going.

And I don't think I'm alone in this, either, in the discovery of the story that I myself am living. I think others do this in their own time, too. For so many of the people who've been reading me have also been talking to me, letting me in on what about my story connects to them, and how they welcome the words that articulate their own.

But in contemplating my own tale, I've come to understand that oftentimes the stories we tell ourselves can be limiting. It can be compelling to identify with only one and then stick with it. The outline may be complete, and it may even be fleshed out with a good bit of drama and some colorful characters, too. But, of course, the ending is then always the same, especially if it's autobiographical.

So while comfort can be found in telling myself the same story over and over, after a while I realize it's probably time for a new one, for something unwritten.

The other night, I attended a Rocket yoga class. I've come to love this style of yoga born from Ashtanga. It's sequential and linear, and it's become a part of my story three times a week. This one I don't mind rereading, and its pages are well worn from multiple practices.

I arrive on the late side and am the last to stand at the top of my mat to await the instructor's narrative. I know how it begins, but tonight the words are different. We're told that we'll instead be practicing Budokon, a mix of yoga and martial arts, another story altogether.

The practice is intense and different. Where Rocket is linear, Budokon is circular. I can't anticipate any of it, and each pose requires a new and concentrated effort. At the end, we rest in Savasana, the final pose.

Tonight, you got something you didn't expect, the instructor says. *Check in with yourselves to see how that feels.*

And I realize it feels pretty good.

Savasana is followed by a request to turn onto our right sides, pulling our knees into a fetal position. This part of the practice symbolizes rebirth, and all of the adults in the room curl up like newborns before rising to a seated position.

And as I roll onto my side, I have a thought. Rolling to the right is like turning to a blank page, and this can be done at any time, at the end of class or even in the middle of a shoe store. And it occurs to me that all of us are not just the stories we tell ourselves. We also get to be our unwritten stories.

And for me, it's the practice that provides the hope for whatever might be written next.

In closing, I place my hands at forehead center and join the others in bowing forward, thanking the teacher within by sharing the word, *Namaste.*

And as is so often the case, I am filled with so much gratitude that it takes a moment to come up from my bow. I linger there, thankful for finally finding the voice to my story, for having the space to reread it as often as I do, and for the chance to write a new one, too.

Truth 2

Self-belief can be enhanced
when self-worth is recognized.

Validation

If I can reach the stars, pull one down for you, shine it on my heart, so you could see the truth ...

~CHANGE THE WORLD, ERIC CLAPTON

It's not always easy to tell the truth.

You can't find the truth anywhere but in yourself.

These were the instructor's words as we lay in Pigeon pose the other night at yoga.

You can't find it in a book. You can't find it in your teacher. You can't find it in anybody else.

I must admit his words brought me up short. If the truth is inside of me, then I want to know exactly where!

Yoga teaches that the body stores emotions and even past traumas. It has taken me a while to buy into this, but I have to admit that the practice does sometimes get emotional. So, maybe there is something to say about the truth literally residing somewhere in there.

But that would mean I'd have to believe there is actual anger in my quads, emotions in my hips, and real love in my heart. And, if that's so, then what's in my arms, my belly, and my back?

And, if the truth is inside of me, then why can't I always access it?

I can see other people's truths so clearly. As far back as I can remember, people have come to me for perspective, clarity and advice.

Most recently, I was reacquainted with a friend who stopped mid-sentence to exclaim, *Wait! Are you someone to whom people come and tell things?* That same week, another friend stopped mid-tears to ask if I had some kind of background in psychology. I don't.

And at work I have a chair in my office across from my desk that gets a lot of traffic. It's called the trouble seat and is used by others who come to unload and ask for advice. *I knew you'd have the answer!* one such visitor said.

How is it that I can so easily see someone else's truth but not always my own?

Yoga ties the physical with the emotional by teaching about the chakras, or energy centers, located along the spine. There are seven, and they spin in a wheel-like fashion if all is going well spiritually, emotionally, and physically.

Supposedly, emotions can block the chakras, and it's the yoga poses, or asanas, that unblock them and get the energy flowing once more.

The chakras are lined up like this:

- The first chakra, the Root Chakra, is located at the base of the spine and is tied to our most innate needs, like survival.

- The second chakra is the Sacral Chakra and is located under the belly button. It's tied to our desires for pleasure and well-being.

- The third chakra is the Solar Plexus Chakra. It's located above the stomach and has to do with self-esteem.

- The fourth chakra is the Heart Chakra and is, of course, located at the center of the chest. This one is all about love.

- The fifth chakra is the Throat Chakra. It's at the throat and is tied to communication and truth.

- The sixth chakra is the Third Eye Chakra, located at the center of the forehead. It has to do with intuition.

- The seventh chakra, the Crown Chakra, is located at the top of the head and is connected to our spirituality.

If this energetic set-up is to be believed, then there is certainly a lot more going on in our bodies than just blood flowing and organs working.

But even knowing all this, I still don't know how X marks the spot when it comes to locating my truth. Mostly, I think I am pretty solid, but I know I can sometimes be thrown for a loop, by others or even myself.

Before yoga, I had become so much more of a closed person. I don't know how the practice opened me up, but somehow it did. Perhaps the practice really did get my wheels spinning.

And now I think that when I look to others or others look to me, we are really just on a quest for validation of what we already know to be true. Perhaps good advice really is just about helping each other see inside to the truth that's already there.

If this is so, then I get it when the instructor says that no one has anyone else's answers. The search for mine happens mostly on my mat, and I don't think it's ending anytime soon.

Expansion

I want to live. I want to give. I've been a miner for a heart of gold.

~HEART OF GOLD, NEIL YOUNG

Giving is a good thing.

It has positive connotations, especially during the holiday season, but also all year round.

It's good to give of our time, our talents, ourselves. But, when giving comes easily, other challenges can arise.

For me, giving is so much in my nature that receiving can actually be difficult, and this ironic concept was brought home to me during one of my yoga practices.

I was in a new class at a place where I don't often practice. I thought it would be good for me to just arrive at a place where I knew no one, where I could be anonymous and keep to myself.

Within moments, though, a very handsome and happy man opened his mat next to mine and introduced himself. My plan already thwarted, we chatted for a while, and the class began.

We were in Triangle pose, or Trikonasana.

To me, Trikonasana is aptly named; it is tricky. It looks easy enough and is definitely a pretty pose, and I especially like the way we glide into it. I turn my body to the side of the room and straddle my legs with my arms out to each side, a standing starfish on the mat. I look over my back shoulder, press my hip back in the same direction and slide my torso forward in the other before tilting to reach my toe.

The weird thing, though, is that this pose always feels a little funny, and I know that means something more is going on.

Expand your arms, the instructor says. *And now expand your chest. Look to the sky and release your heart upward.*

All this in the pretty pose of Trikonasana?

I try to expand the space between my shoulders while leaning sideways and looking up at my hand that reaches for the sky. I try to twist open my torso while leaning back and aiming my heart toward the ceiling.

Create space. Make some room for what this practice has to offer, the instructor continues. *There is so much to take in. See what you can receive.*

I never knew Trikonasana was work. And I never knew receiving was work. I am conscious of making a strong foundation from the hips down while simultaneously opening from the waist up.

One thing I receive right then and there is clarity.

My mind travels not so far back to a time when I was told that, as a giver, I have to actually learn how to receive.

I am often told nice things, both by the very good people in my life and by strangers. It brings me up short each time, and I am always surprised to hear them. No one on the outside can really tell that some hard times have left their marks on the inside, making the opening to receive such niceties that much smaller.

The class continues the flow as the instructor continues to speak. She speaks of how we are all very lucky, very blessed. She says we are lucky to be in the class that night and to experience all that is on offer.

She broadens this thought by saying that life itself has so much to offer, and that we should make some space to take in every blessing. Through the yoga, I feel so open, physically and mentally, that it is easy to receive these words.

At the end of the practice, my neighboring yogi looks over at me.

You are so strong and beautiful, he says.

Surprised, I let myself receive his words, too.

Confidence

Sail on silver girl. Sail on by. Your time has come to shine. All your dreams are on their way.

~BRIDGE OVER TROUBLED WATERS, SIMON AND GARFUNKEL

I am supposed to find my swag in yoga.

Really, I never knew what it was or where it was or even that I was supposed to be looking for it. What I was looking for was how to drop into a backbend from standing, and the instructor was doing his best to help.

I was given lots of direction to find this pose. I was told to look to my quads for my foundation, to my core for my strength, to my straight arms for my landing. Sometimes it felt like I was almost there, and other times it felt incredibly far away.

One night, I was surely lost. I needed lots of help going back and even more coming up. Any progress I had made in the past months of trying seemed to have disappeared.

Where's your swag?! the instructor demanded.

The practice room was hot, and I was a little dizzy from the drop-backs, so I just looked at him and remembered silently that I knew about swag. It was the goods in the gift bags at celebrity events! But what did that have to do with the drop-backs?

It was obvious he couldn't hear me in my head because he looked back at me and told me what was what.

You don't know what swag is? He didn't even comment on the gift bags but instead did a little strut in place and announced, *That's your swag! You gotta get your swag back!*

This insightful instructor has a good sense of humor, but he wasn't joking.

This swag was some serious stuff, and I was supposed to learn something here. Something that would help me drop back, and something that would help me drop in.

So here's what I've learned so far. Swag is the equivalent of confidence, and I can't just reach in a bag and find it. It's about self-belief, the kind you have to have in order to strut in place. It lives in the core, and sometimes it's home and sometimes it's not. And sometimes a deep breath can bring it back.

And, as with the practice itself, it takes work. I have to cultivate this self-belief, and I think the yoga poses help me do that. We're taught that the poses are like any obstacles, and how we face them is how we get through them.

And it's in this way that I learn a lot about myself on the mat, and such understanding makes room for some self-compassion which, in turn, nurtures my confidence. This direct relationship between my practice and my confidence is what helps me to progress. When my confidence is up, I sail through the practice. And when there's no wind in my sails, I'm a little at sea and have to work all the more on the mat.

At one point, I injured my hand being careless in the drop-backs. It has since healed, but it's made me shy away from practicing them. Even so, the other night, I was back at it. And when the instructor stepped up to dip me back, I told him I was scared, even with his assist.

Okay, he said. *So let's face that fear. Let's do a Lion's Breath together.* He opened his mouth, stuck out his tongue and breathed out a loud, *AHHHHHHHH!*

He didn't know my swag was out for the evening, so I only opened my mouth for a little exhale.

Come on! he said.

I hate Lion's Breath and told him so. It's supposed to be a release of energy and heat, but it makes me feel self-conscious. I think it's the part about sticking out my tongue and making a ridiculously big noise. Who knew you had to be confident to do so?

It took four tries before I finally stuck out my tongue and matched his loud exhale. And, wouldn't you know, that self-belief came right back home? It lifted my arms and, with his assist, gave me the confidence to drop right back and the same to rise right up again.

Step Up

I just take one step closer to you. And even when I've fallen down, my heart says follow through.

~ONE STEP CLOSER TO YOU, MICHAEL FRANTI & SPEARHEAD

Step to the top of your mats.

This is what the instructor says at the beginning of most every yoga class.

I hear this so much that it's automatic to simply step to the top when I'm told. I can be finishing a conversation, coming up from a seat or coming down from a stretch. It doesn't matter. Everything stops, my mind clears, and I step to the top.

But last week, I heard something else.

Step to the top of your mats, the instructor announced.

And when I did so, my mind, on its own accord, suddenly responded in silence, *Reporting for duty!*

I've never really had a thought surprise me. I usually know what I'm thinking about. But on that day, my response was as automatic as my step to the top. And even though no one could hear my mind speak out, everyone else reported for duty, too.

If you asked me, I'd answer aloud that I practice yoga to stay in shape, the kind of shape that takes all forms. The practice helps keep me fit physically, mentally and spiritually.

But now I know there is another reason. It's the reason my mind stated, even though that in itself sort of makes me question the state of my mind! Truly, though, practicing has now become my duty, to myself and to those I find around me.

Going to yoga is how I have my own back. It's a vote of confidence in me, by me. It's how I let myself know that I'm worth maintaining, that my body, my mind and my spirit are all worthwhile.

So I'm proud to report for duty, almost daily, because with each day I'm able to see how far I've come in caring for myself.

I took a big detour for a generous portion of my life, throwing the care of my body, mind and spirit off course. Somehow, I let someone other than me navigate, and it's been a very long road back.

Every step to the top of the mat is another step back on track.

The next day comes, and I report for duty as usual. It is a Monday following a long holiday weekend, and I had been uncharacteristically tired for days. The weekend had a strange pace as I practiced and slept and practiced and slept.

At the end of the week's first workday, I stop home to eat and change out of my work clothes. Continuing my weekend pattern, I set the alarm for a 45-minute snooze and fall into a deep sleep before leaving the house.

The evening class is crowded, and there's only one space left for the instructor. The room is hot from the previous class, and the instructor opens the windows to invite in the setting sun and the summer breeze.

Step to the top of your mats, he says.

I automatically take the step, and we're told to place our feet wider than usual and bring our hands to our hearts. We are asked to set an intention or say a prayer or think of anything meaningful.

Every time we're asked to do this, a million things run through my mind, as if I have to figure out something quickly in this very brief moment. Should I bless my children? Should I send good thoughts to someone? Should I say a prayer? Should I, should I, should I?

This night, I decide to send my thoughts to me, which I don't usually do. And, once again, I hear my mind speak on its own accord, this time simply saying the word, *Love.*

And then we're told that we're going to start slowly, and we follow the instructor's motions as he raises his hands to the ceiling before bringing them back to his heart.

I press my hands together and follow them with my eyes, up and overhead, just in time to see a dozen rainbow polka dots splashed across the ceiling, a picture the setting sun has made as it shines through a prism that hangs in the window.

The class moves along at what I find is an unusual pace of patience and power. Somehow, the movements are big and small at the same time. We move carefully and slowly in a way that is powerful and strong. The instructor practices with us while telling us what to do, so we can listen and see at the same time.

Periodically, we are told to stop. After a flow, we are supposed to hold still. We are instructed to take Child's pose. Later, we are told to stay in Down Dog. Still later, we get to choose our stationary pose, and I go into a headstand where I can be still while upside down.

Each time, I'm almost disappointed to stop. I want to keep flowing, and I'm not even aware that I need any sort of break until there is one. Only then do I realize how much effort I've put forth, and it's a welcome rest.

Once we're still, the instructor gives an explanation for why, and the reason is an interesting mix of patience and power, just like the practice.

He says, *You work hard, and you rest hard. Work and rest. Work and rest. You give and give, and then you receive.*

And I realize, then, that this rest between flows is the same as the step to the top of the mat. It's a duty, too. It's what helps to strengthen the body, the mind and the spirit. It's the decision to receive after giving so much.

At the end of the practice, we are asked to bring to mind the intention or prayer that we set at the beginning. I had almost forgotten but remember right away that mine was *Love.*

The practice ends, and I realize this love has already come to pass. Somehow, the movements have fortified me, and I feel solid and worthwhile. I give the instructor a heartfelt hug and tease my friends that it's time to label the studio wall with our names because we'll be back before we know it.

We leave, and I walk to the grocery next door with a friend and hug her, too, telling her I'm honored to know her and love her, too.

And then I turn to shop and see that I'm standing among all the brightly colored fruits and vegetables, their colors a rainbow splashed in front of me like those on the studio ceiling earlier that evening.

And I want to buy them all, because my prayer and my practice worked.

But it's very close to the time to make my way home, because I have to report for duty again tomorrow. So I remember, instead, the mix of patience and power, and I buy just the few things I need, along with a treat or two for *Love.*

Wake-Up Call

But if you never try, you'll never know just what you're worth.

~FIX YOU, COLDPLAY

Wake up to how big you can be in your life.

These were the words of my yoga instructor the other night.

I was at class following my work day, trying to recommit to my workout. Although I had been practicing regularly, I felt my dedication slipping, and my body felt it, too. That evening, I unrolled my mat more to wake up my muscles and less to wake up my mind.

As usual, though, yoga gave me something more than I was seeking.

Earlier that day on the drive to work, I had received a morning pep talk from my very patient mother. I was having what I call a short-sighted morning where I couldn't see the forest for the trees.

You don't recognize all the things you are capable of, my mother told me.

Somehow, our conversation had veered off into the treacherous terrain of self-doubt, the area I usually keep cordoned off tightly with no access allowed.

You need to give yourself credit for all that you have accomplished and for all that you are able to do, she added.

I arrived at work shortly thereafter. It was quiet, and I grabbed some coffee and hopped on an email exchange with a colleague familiar with my daily work, my writing and the bit of work I do with my daughter, among other things.

I don't know how you do it all, she exclaimed in her email.

What is it I do? I wondered but didn't write. *I only do what I do!*

It's not in my nature to take such inventory; however, twice that morning, I had heard the same thing, a clear signal to pay attention to the message.

Once at evening yoga, though, the morning seems like a long time ago.

We are in Crescent Lunge with one leg forward and bent at the knee, and the other shooting straight back, long and strong. Arms reach high alongside the ears and energy sparks out of the fingertips.

Reach up, the instructor says. *Grow long through the crown of the head and reach for the sky. You can grow in yoga, just like you can in life.*

I reach high and look at the ceiling, thinking about the annual physical I had after only a few months of yoga. I had grown a little bit! Apparently, it is true that you can grow in yoga just like you can in life!

The instructor tells us to tilt back, grow big and explore what we can see. I reach back, lifting my gaze and tracking the ceiling toward the back wall. I stretch myself as best I can, growing to the edge of comfort.

Later, we stand in Tree pose, one foot to the ground with the other pressed to the opposite inner thigh. In Tree, we are supposed to grow in opposite directions, with energy pressing downward through the standing leg and upward through the crown of the head. I hold the pose for a few beats before interlacing my fingers and pushing my arms down before raising them up.

Again, I lift my gaze and track the ceiling toward the back wall. Again, I stretch myself as best I can, growing to the edge of comfort.

The practice is hard but in a good way. My muscles wake up, and my body is challenged. I reach the end feeling accomplished and confident, and the day's message of self-awareness hits home.

It seems so easy to recognize the abilities of others, but it's often so much more difficult to recognize my own.

I roll up my mat, grateful to my mother and my colleagues for pushing me to see myself, and grateful to the practice for making me tilt even further for a better view.

Stillness

How could I possibly be inconspicuous when my flow is [so] ridiculous?

~I'LL BE AROUND, CEE-LO GREEN

I was at an evening yoga class with a guest instructor who arrived with a great big welcome, his greeting warming the room, and his smile inviting many in return.

This is a Level Two class, he announced. *So what would you like to work on?*

With each answer, he jokingly upped the ante, saying, *Oh, hips? That's a 3.23 class! Inversions? That's a 5.67 class! Backbends? That's a 10.789 class!*

He asked us what we wanted and got us laughing when we answered, promising us a high energy class and lifting us with that of his own before landing the room in a quiet meditation with a poem and a chant.

I was happy to be there, sitting next to a friend who was leaving town and among others I knew, as well. I felt cozy as evening fell outside the windows, darkening the room in a stillness filled with the rhythmic voice of the instructor.

I didn't really take in any of the poem or understand the chant; rather, it was as if the sound of his words blanketed my busy thoughts, tucking them away and settling me into a stillness usually found in the final resting pose of Savasana.

It felt as if we were beginning at the end, but then we suddenly jumped to the middle! The instructor popped up from his seated position, turned on the music and moved us directly into Boat pose, a pose that works on the abdominals and is usually found halfway through the class. After more core work, we moved into an early Crow pose, balancing on our hands with our knees tucked as high above the backs of our arms as possible.

And then we started to flow, and he even threw in a few handstands between warrior poses. He danced to the music and bounced around the room, adjusting us here and there and singing along, too, his energy lifting us again before landing the room in the quiet of Warrior II.

And there we held the pose.

Along with the others, I settled into stillness once more, but this time with much more effort as he implored us to take the pose even deeper. He ran through a checklist, asking us to see every part of our bodies as he outlined the view of our arms, our legs, our bellies and more.

I even want you to see the backs of your knees, he said. *I want you to see your blind spots.*

There is something about expending lots of energy while being still. Somehow, everything seems to make sense in the stillness, like understanding the words to a chant without any knowledge of the language.

And it's in this way that I saw myself as instructed, and I at once remembered an astrologer telling me the stars were such that I should *walk the King's Highway*. When I asked for an explanation, I was told that I was not supposed to sit on the side, that I was meant to be seen.

My muscles were working hard, and I felt so alert that it seemed as if I could see out of every pore. And I was so still that I found myself strong enough to look at my blind spots and to understand that it's okay to be seen. I even pictured the backs of my knees.

We held the pose still longer, and the energy was as high as we had been in our handstands earlier in the practice.

I want you to do this pose as if it's the last yoga pose you'll ever do, he said.

This brought some giggles to the room, but he held his ground in much the same way as we held the pose.

Seriously, he said, countering with his smile. *This could be the last time you'll ever do yoga. There is no tomorrow.*

And so there I was, standing still in what turned out to be the *Just Now*, where nothing is hidden if you are brave enough to look. It was a liberating place to be, among my fellow warriors with no tomorrow, doing all that mattered in the moment, and seeing all of myself from the inside out.

We broke the pose and flowed once more, the music never having stopped. The instructor continued his beat around the room, singing and dancing and asking us to see ourselves, and somehow getting us to do just that by sending us from stillness to flow to stillness to flow.

Soon after, we moved into Reverse Side Angle. I stepped one foot in front of the other and twisted to my left, placing my right hand on the mat and reaching the other to the ceiling. And as I turned my torso to the side, my eyes passed along the window, and I saw a single star, like an eye in the sky blinking down at me.

I stared at the star, and it gazed back, each of us seeing the other in the clarity of the stillness that was the *Just Now*.

But before I knew it, the flow was upon us again, and I averted my eyes, flowing all the way to the end of the class until the room finally settled into its sweat and its breath and another poem and another chant. And I lay there in the stillness against the rhythm of the words, and I felt free in the bravery of being bare enough to be seen by even me.

And when it came time to leave, I wanted to thank the instructor. And so, even though I knew he knew there were no tomorrows, I asked him to please come back again as if there were.

Open Face

Sweat

Influence

Sun Spot

Rain

Movement

<u>Truth 3</u>

Space for joy can be created
when inhibitions are released.

Open Face

So don't be afraid to let them show - your true colors. True colors are beautiful like a rainbow.

~TRUE COLORS, CYNDI LAUPER

Sometimes I'm invited to help my daughter with her work in New York City and, each time I go, I pack up my yoga mat and together we attend as many classes as our schedule allows.

Although I am early on in what I think of as my *working-out days*, my daughter has been cross training for many years. She takes dance classes, goes to the gym, runs along the East River, practices yoga and more.

I am always amazed that she can just throw her hair up, put on her workout gear and look beautiful before, during, and after her sweat. I even have a memory of one of her school coaches asking me, *How is it she looks like she just got off the runway instead of the soccer field?*

I, on the other hand, would never leave the house without hair and makeup done, much less appear in New York City that way. Having my bangs trimmed has always been key to a good day.

Yoga, however, has changed all that.

My daughter and I arrive at her hot yoga studio in our favorite yoga outfits. I have on my new short shorts and matching sports bra, prepared for the intense heat, and she has on the same. My daughter has a beautiful braid in her hair, and I have on my newly trimmed bangs. We are looking good!

The class opened up and, as we got into the flows, the instructor began to speak about masks and humanity.

Will you show your humanity to another? she asked.

As we practiced, she spoke of how most of us wear a mask during our days, carefully positioning ourselves and presenting only what we want others to see.

She related this to how some of us prepare for yoga by making sure we look our best in outfits that we think look good, by having yoga hairdos that are just so, and even by wearing a little makeup.

Yoga, she said, *strips all that away. We do yoga*, she said, *to remove our masks.*

We sweat. We drip on our neighbors. Our hair falls and gets plastered to our temples and foreheads. Our outfits cling to us with perspiration. Maybe we look a little funny in our poses. Maybe we're not looking so good anymore.

Maybe none of it matters.

Yoga removes your mask, the instructor said. *But do you care? Will you show your humanity to another? Do you dare?*

After the class, we step outside, our bodies actually cooling in the summer evening's heat now that we are out of the hot studio.

There I stood in Union Square in New York City, sweaty, bangs pinned back, whatever makeup once there now gone.

I felt amazing.

Let me take your picture, my daughter said. *Your humanity is showing.*

Sweat

You're once, twice, three times a lady.

~THREE TIMES A LADY, LIONEL RICHIE

It's the best part of my day, my evening yoga practice.

I arrive dressed in work heels, work makeup, and work hair. I grab the keys to the changing room and peel off the day, putting on my yoga pants and top and taking off the shoes that I'd had on since early that morning.

It had been a long day, but something was still missing.

I had not yet sweat!

Before yoga, I had never worked out. I was raised to be a lady, and being a lady and sweating never quite equated for me. And the last thing I would have ever wanted to do, at the beginning or at the end of a day, was exercise.

But the sweat! I can't even explain how much I love it! How good it feels to work my body hard, so every muscle is engaged, so the sweat pours.

On this particular evening, I am late to yoga. I had visited a relative in the hospital and had sat with him for a bit after work. I didn't want to rush my visit; my whole family was concerned for him.

I arrive at the studio with barely time to spare. After changing, I enter the practice area to find the music already playing and the class already started. I squeeze my mat into a space at the very edge of the crowded room. I am far from my usual spot, and I can't even see the clock. But I care not a lick, happy to be on my mat and more than content to join in.

Before long, we are flowing, and so is the sweat. How did we get here so fast? I am always so unaware of the time going by. It rains on my mat as I am brought to that zone by the music and the instruction.

Before I know it, my arms are wet, my back is wet, my face is wet and so is my hair.

In each vinyasa, or transition, I pop into a handstand and set my intention on my uncle in the hospital, holding the pose as long as possible while watching the drips of sweat speckle my mat below.

In college, my sorority dedicated a song to me, Lionel Richie's *Once, Twice, Three Times a Lady*. I think about this when I am upside down and feel the sweat dripping *up* my nose.

Doing yoga has been so completely liberating. I started out so very self-conscious, and now I simply just am not. I don't care what's going on with my hair, if I have to double up my shirt to cool off, or what's with my leftover makeup.

Before I know it, we are in the final resting position of Savasana, or Corpse pose. We just lie there on our backs, listening to the music and cooling off.

Not being near the clock, the end has caught me by surprise. I had thought we were only halfway through! I am soaked and ready for more.

We end the class in the usual manner, in a seated position with our hands in prayer.

Take in some positive energy, the instructor says, *and release what you don't need.*

I feel calm yet energized, cool yet hot. I think about white stars falling on my recuperating relative and inhale what I imagine to be the same.

Reluctantly, I roll up my mat and change my clothes.

On the way out, I run into another yogi on her way in. With her greeting, she mistakes me for the lady I am trying so hard *not* to be.

Look at you! she exclaims. *Did you even sweat?*

•

Influence

Hear my words that I might teach you. Take my arms that I might reach you.

~SOUNDS OF SILENCE, SIMON AND GARFUNKEL

There are people in my life who influence me, some to whom I'm very close, others who are really just passing through.

It never really strikes me that I myself might be in a position to influence others. Turns out, I am!

And that position is upside down.

Being upside down has become a highlight of my day. The inversion segment of my yoga class isn't really that long but, for me, it's the part of class that's the most fun.

During this time, we can practice anything we want as long as our feet are above our hearts. Shoulder Stand. Handstand. Forearm Stand. Headstand.

It's our choice, and the instructor either walks around and helps us or leaves us alone on the chance that we might topple over with the attention.

When I first started yoga, the thought of going upside down felt silly. I was self-conscious. It was one thing to know I could do a headstand; it was another to do one in public. Even my children knew I could do a headstand, and I had done one on Skype for my daughter and her college roommates a few years earlier, but that's really another topic.

So at yoga, in the beginning, I would just rest on my back and hoist my hips and extend my legs to the sky with my hands on the small of my back in Shoulder Stand. And I would wait for the segment to be over.

Then came the day when my daughter and I had a private lesson. I was completely at ease with just the instructor and my daughter and, when it came time to try an inversion, I moved to the wall and did a headstand.

One, two, three, I was upside down!

In the months that follow, my daughter conquers her fear of going upside down. My son's turn comes next. Both live out of town and, one day, my son calls to say, *Today, before work, I just popped out of bed and went into a headstand!*

The sphere of influence widens, and I start receiving more news of my children and their various friends upside down.

There were my daughter and her friends in Central Park, upside down. My younger cousin in a headstand at a Passover Seder. My daughter's friend who announces he can do a headstand and, soon thereafter, proves it at a party. There comes a photo of my son one night upside down in his work clothes, tie hanging in his face, the caption reading: *Banker in a Headstand.*

One day, I receive a text message. It's a picture of a woman in a headstand. Turns out, she is the mother of one of my daughter's friends and used to be a gymnast. Summertime brings more e-photos of three of my daughter's friends in headstands, poolside.

Today, I can stand on my forearms, Pincha Mayurasana. I can finally pop into a handstand with a wall nearby, and sometimes without, and I can transition from a headstand into Forearm Stand.

I guess the biggest lesson I've learned is not that I've accomplished these inversions, but that I've moved past any self-consciousness in doing so. And that's what my children picked up on. It's what made it okay for them to try, too, and for their cousins and for their friends and even, to my surprise, for the mothers of their friends!

And who knows who else? Turns out, going upside down impacts more than just the person on her head.

Yoga conquered my self-consciousness. It took some time, but ultimately the practice let my body take precedence over my mind.

And this has been be quite liberating and, apparently, quite catching.

Sun Spot

Good day sunshine. I feel good in a special way ...

~GOOD DAY SUNSHINE, THE BEATLES

It's Sunday morning, and I open my mat near the window along the back wall of the studio.

It's a winter day, and the sky is blue and cloudless. It's cold, but the sun is shining, and I am glad my parking spot is several blocks away. It feels good to walk in the early morning quiet, only a few others out and about on this bright and beautiful day.

The class before ours is crowded, and the room gets heated, so those leaving pry open the windows in their wake. I keep on my long sleeves while setting up, chatting with some of the others and trying to warm up my mat, still cold from the night it spent in the car.

This class is Rocket yoga. It's challenging and strenuous and one of my favorites. It's an interesting mix of people and an interesting mix of flows and inversions and arm balances. I am pushed to my limits each time.

The instructor enters the room and closes the windows against the sunny chilled air and starts the music. The demanding sequence is set against a soundtrack that I would call easy listening. It's definitely Sunday morning music, even if the workout is anything but.

Come to the top of your mats, she says, and all the lounging yogis slowly stand at attention for the start of the practice.

We reach up and there follows the flow of several Sun A's, after which we flow into several Sun B's.

My eyes follow my arms as they lift to the ceiling, then look down for the fold to the floor. We continue through our vinyasas, from Chaturanga (low push-up) to Urdhva Mukha (Upward Facing Dog) to Adho Mukha (Downward Facing Dog).

The instructor calls out the Sanskrit words, and her voice becomes as easy listening as the music. I watch our shadows flow across the floor as we flow through the sun postures.

It doesn't take long before I realize that the shadow I think is mine is really that of my neighbor's to the right, and that mine is really that on the mat of my neighbor's to the left.

It appears the sun from the window behind me has moved us each over one spot. It shines on my back and on that of my neighbor, making a great big sun spot that stretches out beyond our mats and across the floor, window panes and all.

We move into the part of the practice with the twists, rinsing to one side and then to the other. The music has made its way into my head, and I have to concentrate on breathing and not singing as I place one hand to the mat and the other to the ceiling before binding and twisting to the side.

With each twist to the right, I face the window that's behind my neighbor and me. We look back over our shoulders as our hips face forward and our torsos twist open.

Each time I do this, I close my eyes in the face of the sun. Its heat matches the heat I am building on the inside, and I let it wash over me.

And then my mind drifts to memories of our wonderful chocolate Labrador, Chelsea. She adored the sun spots, too. She was a special dog, a true member of the family. Sweet, beautiful, kind and gentle, I would swear she understood full sentences.

We chose her from a large litter, but it was really as if she had chosen us. At first sight, she came right over and lay across the tops of our shoes. I carried her home and, each night after work, when I made a salad at the sink, Chelsea would lay on the tops of my feet.

When she was older, she graduated from our feet to the sun spots. I could tell the time of day by where she lay as she made her way around the house with the sun.

Our dog is no longer with us, but she often comes to mind as she did this day when I was lucky enough to have the Sunday morning sun at yoga.

We enter the final portion of the practice, and I do my best to land in Hanumanasana, or the splits. I never quite got these in my teens nor ever imagined I'd be trying them again now.

We face the back wall, and I grab two blocks and place them on either side, lowering myself to the mat. I put my face up to the sun and close my eyes, listening to the music, willing my body down between the blocks.

I turn to my neighboring yogi, and there she is, no blocks, in full splits, seated comfortably on her mat. Her arms are lifted above her head with her palms pressed together, and her heart is lifted, too, as she bends back in the spotlight of the sun.

I lean over, interrupting her pose.

We are taking your picture after class, I said. *There, like that, in the sun spot.*

Afterward, we do just that. It's a beautiful picture, and she looks beautiful in it. And she's excited to see her pose captured in a photograph.

But to me, the photo captures even more. It captures the sun spot.

It washes over her, and she looks the way I feel - special - when soaked in the Sunday morning sun at yoga.

Rain

Some people feel the rain. Others just get wet.

~BOB MARLEY

It's been raining. It's been raining for two days. And I've always loved the rain.

When I was a little girl on rainy days at camp, my friends and I would pile into the social hall with our sleeping bags and watch old movies. My favorites were the Gene Kelly movies, *Anchors Away* and *Singin' in the Rain*. I worked for weeks on his move where he carries his black umbrella under the lampposts and clicks his heels in midair, off to one side and then to the other.

I love the rain in the morning, and I love the rain at night. If I'm inside, I can hear its soothing sound through the roof, on the skylights, and on the windows.

It's even been raining at yoga.

Rain has never kept me home and, apparently, it didn't keep anyone else home the other night, either, when I found myself dripping among almost 70 people at yoga. We lined up outside so those in the previous class could leave and, one by one, we waited to be checked in to enter.

Most people duck for cover in the rain, but I was happy to stand there.

Anne, come in, we've got you!

I heard my name called and looked up to see the front desk ushering me in from outside. I think they thought it was a favor, bringing me in from the rain!

The studio was packed with people. Like two schools of fish, the lobby area seemed to swim in opposite directions. Those drenched wet from the practice moved right to change and leave while those of us drenched wet from the rain moved left to enter.

And that was when I felt the first drop on my head. It seemed the rain had made its way inside!

We set our mats close together, the room already hot and humid. I was not in my usual spot, near the front on the left and toward the door. The claustrophobia set in just a bit, and I briefly wished I was again outside in the open air among the raindrops.

The flow began and, before the sweat even set in, I saw wet specks on my mat. I assumed these were from the man next to me, sweating onto my mat. This happens at this studio. We practice so close together.

We flow into a low push-up. Another drop, this time on my neck. I realize the water is coming from the ceiling. We flow into Warrior I, and the man next to me whispers an apology for sweating on my mat. But now I know the rain has followed us into the studio.

Before I know it, I am lost to the practice and creating my own rain. I have watered my own mat and have started to slip and slide. I spread my towel overtop for grip. It is so hot that I'm grateful each time the ceiling rains.

We finish the class. We are all of us wet, the windows are wet, the floor is wet, my towel is wet.

I put on my overclothes, say goodbye and step out into the rain. I see others duck their heads and dash, but I take a few steps and stop to put my face up to the sky. I let the rain fall on me, looking up at the drops, and then close my eyes to feel it on my face.

My water bottle is the only thing that's dry at the moment, and I make my usual stop at one of the local shops that keeps some cucumber water on the counter. Everyone inside is smiling. And tonight strawberries are floating in the pitcher instead of cucumbers.

It's a good day. It's a good night.

The rain is lit by the lampposts, and I step through the puddles just like Gene Kelly, only I'm carrying my yoga bag instead of his black umbrella.

Snow is supposed to come tomorrow, but that's another story.

For now, I make my way back to the car, trying hard not to let the raindrops miss me.

Movement

A little sweat ain't never hurt nobody. Don't just stand there on the wall.
Everybody just move your body. (Jump, jump, jump, jump, jump!)

~MOVE YOUR BODY, BEYONCE

From one day to the next, I look forward to yoga.

It's been some time since I first stepped into the studio, and I never tire of it. I like preparing to go. I like being there. I like the workout.

And, in turn, I like whatever it is I am doing afterward. The aftereffects of each class stay with me until the next class, and so I go as often as I can.

It's a good place, and it puts me in a good space.

I can't exactly pinpoint what it is about yoga that clicks with me, but something definitely does. And I don't think it's anything new in me to which it connects but rather to something seemingly age old, perhaps from the time I was little and maybe from even before.

In one of my vinyasa classes, we were in a flow, moving among many different poses. We flowed from Warrior I to Warrior II to High Lunge. We swept our arms down and back and raised them up again. We leaned back and spread our arms open and then swept them down again.

The music played, my body flowed, and my mind did, too, back to when I was six or seven or eight years old in ballet class.

We moved into Standing Split and then brought our feet together for a forward fold. We lifted halfway and folded again and then flowed into Warrior II once more. We straightened our front leg and flowed into Triangle pose.

My body reached forward and my mind reached back, and I so clearly remembered myself in my black leotard and pink tights doing *The Fun Step*. This happened at the end of ballet class when the teacher would map out a pattern of steps across the room and change up the music. We would skip and hop, one at a time, traveling on a diagonal from one corner to the other.

I loved it. I vividly remember looking down to trace the pattern with my feet but having such difficulty seeing my toes beyond my little girl's stomach!

We flowed back to Warrior II and then sailed right into Half Moon. I bent my back leg and grabbed my ankle for a bind in a sideways backbend.

As a little girl, I never wanted to go to ballet. It was scheduled on Saturday mornings when I was allowed to watch television, and I didn't want to do anything but watch *H.R. Puff and Stuff*. But I was always happy at the end of class when the good music played, and we flowed freely with *The Fun Step*.

After class, I would always hang back to watch the older girls dancing jazz, wishing to be one of them, dancing more freely and always to better music.

Ultimately, my mother caved, and I left the ballet scene only to wish in my teenage years that I hadn't. I filled the gap with other dance classes and dance squads throughout my middle and high school years and, in college, I fulfilled my physical education requirement with a dance class, too.

We moved through our vinyasas and repeated the sequence on the other side, moving from one big motion to the next. The good music played, and I sailed freely between the poses as I followed the instructions that made up the flows of the class.

There has always been something about movement and music that works for me and, somehow, yoga connects me to that. The music and the movement take my body and mind through a moving meditation, and that's what I think keeps me coming back.

One instructor makes sense of it another way. He says, *Moving like this is how we are moved.*

Ironically, in his class, there is no music. Instead, in his class, we move to the beat of our breath.

Regardless, for me it's all the same, because, really, I'm just doing *The Fun Step* all over again, only this time I can see my toes.

Soul Searching

Unfolding

Carl Jung

Anger

Grief

Uncertainty

Truth 4

Anxieties can be faced
when emotions are uncovered.

Soul Searching

Lend me your eyes, I can change what you see, but your soul you must keep totally free. Awake my soul.

~AWAKE MY SOUL, MUMFORD AND SONS

Yoga is supposed to be mindful and meditative. Its transformative effects are supposed to infiltrate the body, mind and spirit.

To me, this means it should touch my soul. But sometimes I can lose sight of this as I focus my attention on advancing my practice.

My soul must have been very sleepy the other morning because I ignored my alarm and closed my eyes instead of going to my morning vinyasa class. This was so unusual for me, but I felt bone tired. My body, mind and spirit seemed to need some more time under the covers.

It was a Monday and, as always, the first workday of the week went by fast. Once home, I signed up for the evening class to make up for the morning miss, changed into my yoga clothes, took one look at my bed and climbed back in!

I set the alarm for a 20-minute snooze and soon thereafter was on my mat.

My neighboring yogi was doing his warmups and chatting with me as I just stood there, afraid that if I sat down, I would call it a day. I told him how tired I was but that I knew the practice would wake me up.

He replied that for him the practice removes all stress. After, he said, he feels calm and peaceful.

When you are working that hard, there is just no space for anything else, he told me.

I told him that, instead of feeling calm and peaceful after my practice, I often feel completely energized. If I were a runner, I'd likely run somewhere afterward.

Any mindful and meditative part of the practice is simply a surprising side effect for me. It pulls at my soul strings, but I find myself somewhat resistant.

Lately, I seem to be feeling stuck. I want to move forward faster, and I'm asking the instructor how to progress, what's next, and why I can't achieve the new inversions that were only recently introduced.

Your practice is very strong, is the answer I get. *You need to relax about it.*

This is not what I want to hear. I want to know where to tuck my elbow in order to extend from Side Crow into Fallen Angel.

I went home that night wide awake from the practice. After being so tired all day, for hours I could not fall asleep.

The transformative effects of yoga seem to come unbidden, seeping their way in, welcome or not. They want to wake me up and keep me awake until I *get it*. And that night I wondered if trying to *up* my practice through advancing my poses might just be my way of resisting exactly that.

I know that adding in some meditation would probably go a long way, but I have some resistance to that, too.

I don't always want to think about what yoga sometimes makes me think about. Sometimes it is shouting at me to pay attention, and I think sleeping in on my practice that morning might just have been my way of covering my ears.

Admittedly, the practice has made me face up to some things that I long ago put aside and at which I've become quite expert at avoiding. But now I think opening up to myself in this way might just give my soul some much needed space. And if I am brave enough, maybe I could find some room in this new space for something more.

For now, though, I am just going to figure out where to put my elbows so that I can invert myself properly. I want to go from Crow to Fallen Angel; from Lizard to Cheek Stand, from Peacock to Chin Stand.

Hopefully, if I can get my body to do this, my soul will simply follow suit.

Unfolding

And when the night is cloudy, there is still a light that shines on me. Shine on until tomorrow. Let it be.

~LET IT BE, THE BEATLES

Sometimes there are situations about which I can't figure out how I feel until they are over.

I can have delayed reactions where my anxiety level skyrockets, and that never serves me well. I wind up taking a break from everything, including yoga.

Anxiety never leads me in the right direction. And taking a break from yoga, however short, is always the wrong direction.

After one such break, I returned to my yoga class, and it went by in five minutes flat. I had really missed being there. And at the end, as usual, the instructor imparted a few words of wisdom, words that I wished I'd had the chance to hear earlier.

Think of a situation you were in not long ago, and think of how you could have handled it better, he told the class. *Maybe you could have handled it differently by letting the situation peacefully unfold.*

When I first started yoga, I wanted to excel quickly: reverse bind, Bird of Paradise, backbend, high split with no hands on the mat. I couldn't do any of that, though, and the practice was gradual.

The instruction was gradual, too. Sometimes we would spend at least a month or more working on the same things, even if it was only a step or two toward the full expression of a pose.

At times I'm finally able to reach full expression, and at times I just cannot. In yoga, I've learned to have patience as I work toward something, and I've been taught that I can get into a deeper expression of a pose by that peaceful unfolding about which the instructor spoke. Trying to jump into final expression is nearly always impossible.

Letting a situation peacefully unfold is not a usual part of my repertoire. It's something I've had to work at, and this work really began when I became a mother so many years ago.

When my children were very little, I was in charge. However, as they grew older, it quickly became apparent that I would have to make room for them as people in their own right, allowing for their own decisions and desires and not just for my own.

I've learned that letting things unfold often involves letting go, and this is a continuing exercise in my life today. I realize now that the best outcomes appear when things work easily. These are usually situations in which I don't have to push too much for anything to happen, situations which I allow to peacefully unfold.

Today, I can do a reverse bind, a Bird of Paradise, a backbend and a high split with no hands on the mat. Even so, I find there still remains a challenge in each of these poses with so many more on which to work. But that's okay, because somehow it's easier to peacefully unfold inside the studio.

There it can happen right on the mat.

The trick is to be able to do this when I leave, because that's what makes it possible to find the peace in those situations where I'd otherwise find the angst.

Carl Jung

Yoga can either improve your mood, or let loose a flood of sufferings of which no sane person ever dreamed.

This, according to The Washington Post, is what psychiatrist Carl Jung thought about yoga.

I look at my yoga practice as a workout. It keeps me in shape. In fact, I only started yoga because I had run out of excuses not to exercise.

Yoga worked fast on my body. I got very toned, very quickly. In a few short months, I saw muscles in my arms, legs and torso for the first time. I even saw a picture of myself in a handstand and realized I had muscles in my back. I went for a medical visit only to have the doctor exclaim about my lack of body fat. All thanks to yoga.

Plus, I was on a yoga high for so long. Every day was a good day, and I saw the positive side of everything.

Indeed, Carl Jung was right. Yoga improved my mood.

When the instructor said that hip openers, like Pigeon pose, released emotions, I sort of doubted that. To me, Pigeon was just a pose where we were prone on our mats with one leg bent and tucked up underneath us. Not too comfortable but a good stretch all the same.

I also sort of doubted when the instructor told me that my quads held anger. What did I have to be angry about? Life was good. I felt good. Yoga was good.

So I would say that, for quite a while, I was in agreement with Jung's first thought, that yoga improves one's mood.

Yoga opened up something in me. Little by little, over a long stretch, the classes sort of melted me, and I felt like I was doing some long overdue healing. I felt strong and spirited for the first time in a long time.

But then something strange happened. All sorts of things came up for me. And I doubted myself greatly, because the difficult feelings that started bubbling up did not seem to mesh with my newfound self and my newfound outlook.

The instructor also told me that backbends were heart openers. I sort of doubted that, too. I was just proud to finally accomplish the pose. I was told that Dancer, a standing backbend, was a heart opener, as well. Boy, I hated those heart openers, and Dancer was the worst!

The more I excelled at the poses, the more so many emotions emerged. And this took me by surprise. Suddenly, it seemed that what I had put behind me was right in front of me. Old wounds and the like were new again. So much of the changing I thought I had done over so many years was brought back into question - by me!

I was surprised to find myself in great shape on the outside but not so much on the inside. And, apparently, the inside does not whip into shape as quickly as the outside.

So I did the only thing I knew to do, and that was to persevere through the poses and even through what they seemed to bring forth. And on some days, it seemed like Carl Jung must have met me when he said that yoga can *let loose a flood of sufferings of which no sane person ever dreamed.*

On those days, I had wanted to quit. Instead, I stayed in it and am glad for it. And now my inside has started to whip into better shape, aligning more with my outside.

As Carl Jung suggested, the impact of the practice can be pretty profound. Luckily, for me, it has served as teacher and healer in one.

Anger

If I stand all alone, will the shadow hide the color of my heart? Blue for the tears, black for the night's fears.

~I DON'T WANT TO TALK ABOUT IT, ROD STEWART

I had been in great spirits of late, and I credited this with my almost daily yoga practice.

I loved the class, my practice and even my mat.

I was seeing the bright side of most things, most days. I was on a yoga high, even on the days I didn't practice.

So imagine my surprise when the instructor told me I was holding anger in my quads.

But I'm not angry, I said, to which he replied that the anger was in my quads.

But what am I angry about? I asked, to which he answered that he could not say, but that it was in my quads.

Well, what am I supposed to do with it? I followed up, to which he answered, *Just do the poses and release it.*

Is that why the poses that hurt the most, especially during the early months of my practice, were always High Lunge, Low Lunge, Runner's Lunge and Warrior III? These are all poses that engage the quad muscles. And I just thought my quads were burning because I had never really exercised, and my thighs were easily and quickly fatigued.

Anger in my quads. This was news to me. Just do the poses and release the energy.

Once upon a time, someone told me that anger serves as a secondary emotion. It covers other emotions like hurt, confusion or sadness.

If I am to be honest, I would have to admit that I don't always recognize when I'm angry. So maybe the instructor was onto something and giving me instruction on more than just yoga.

I'm a single mother, on my own for quite some time. A lot has happened and, if I am to be honest again, I would have to admit that I likely have some anger somewhere inside. Maybe it's deep down, and maybe I don't live in it. Maybe it indeed covers up some hurt, confusion, and sadness.

It's been news to me that yoga is not just a physical practice but also an emotional one. The saving grace, though, is that the practice provides the tools to deal with some of these emotions physically. Through the poses, I gain strength and release energy at the same time. It's as though my body does the work that my mind cannot, and I get cleared out, even though I'm not always aware of any clutter.

And I'm glad for this because now, along with some much stronger quads, have come some openings in some places that I thought were closed for good.

Grief

A kind word. A sweet gesture. A chocolate chip cookie. Nothing grand.

It has never taken much to make me happy.

In college, there was a boy who would bring me dessert in the dining hall and proclaim exactly that.

When I married, we lived well, but I knew in my heart I would have been happy with just some love in a shack.

The other night, someone was celebrating an anniversary of sorts and passed out roses. I was one of the many recipients and was so touched, you would have thought I had been handed a diamond.

Here and there, I find myself the recipient of other peoples' kindnesses. And although it's never any different than what I would do myself, these days, anyone's generosity toward me sort of catches me off guard.

No small gift has been the opportunity to write, and this came about through yoga. A long story short, my practice led to a meeting with an editor who asked me to blog on all things yoga.

Most of my articles are published, but some are stashed in a backlog, maybe never to be posted, ever. These posts I find too revealing. They talk about what I think is my grief.

I am surprised to have come upon such deep grief. How did it get there, especially if I am seemingly so easy to please?

Supposedly, past traumas are stored in our bodies, and it is the yoga poses that release them.

Truly, I thought I had dealt with any traumas long ago; however, now I think not. I think instead I just pushed them down, hiding them so well that I reached this point in time without realizing I had ever even suffered at all. For them to appear now has startled me but, then again, I practice almost every day.

Really, I'm not so sure how well equipped I am to deal with any sort of grief. And I'm most surprised by my inclination to internalize, laying all the blame on the inside.

I am doing my best to fortify myself but, admittedly, at times, I think I have crumbled a bit. But maybe this is just what grieving is? Maybe to grieve is to feel whatever comes up, to not stifle emotions and to not attempt to figure it all out.

Maybe I am not so much crumbling as I am just grieving.

In the past, I never gave grief much credence. I didn't see the strength in it. When encountering difficult times, my goal was always to hunker down, push aside any negative feelings and move right along.

But now there is yoga. And the practice not only uncovers lost wounds but also makes me feel the feelings associated with them. Thank goodness, though, on top of that, the practice also gives me the tools to move through these feelings and not just bury them as I guess I must have years ago.

All this was never an intention. It is just what has come about.

Sometimes after a practice I feel joyous. Sometimes I feel spent. Sometimes at the end, in Pigeon pose, I feel rested, and other times I cannot stop the tears from flowing.

Either way, emotions are moving through me, which is more than I can say was happening before, and I'm thinking that's a good thing.

Uncertainty

How can I be sure in a world that's constantly changing?

~HOW CAN I BE SURE, THE YOUNG RASCALS

We were standing in Pyramid pose.

I was excited to be in a new yoga class. I was ready for a challenge and wanted to learn some new arm balances and inversions and whatever else was on offer.

I felt in fine spirits and in fine form. I placed my mat among some of the yogis I have come to know and admire, happy to see them and always inspired by them.

We stood with our left legs forward and our right legs back. We placed our hands behind our backs in reverse prayer (I grabbed opposite elbows instead as my hands just do not pray this way), and we brought our chins as close as possible to our shins.

With my fine spirits, I folded forward in what I figured was my fine form. Glad to be there with the others, I felt connected as I held the pose.

And that is when the tears appeared.

They were brief. My eyes just welled up without notice, and I had no understanding of why they were there.

Find your center, the instructor said.

She wanted us to push our left hip back and our right hip forward. She wanted us to feel the isometric action.

Next thing I knew, she walked up behind me and adjusted my stance. Turns out, I was not in such fine form, after all. I was realigned into a better but less comfortable position.

You may feel uncertain, she told the class, *but this is your center*.

I blinked quickly to clear my eyes and focused on my body, trying to figure out how I was supposed to be centered if I felt so off balance. And that is when I realized what those tears were all about.

Uncertainty. It's something that's never a good thing for me.

I can easily give myself a hard time if I am doubtful, especially if I find myself perched on a fence and unable to resolve a dilemma. Often I think I am supposed to power through a decision in much the same way as I sometimes power through a pose. But that strategy is not always best.

Yoga has taught me not to power through but instead to sit still and see what might unfold. I've learned that letting things be may involve some uncertainty, but sitting still is the best way to embrace that. In stillness, solutions have a chance to evolve, and I have the chance to face whatever comes about as a result.

I leaned forward over my front knee and pushed those tears away. I concentrated on the scissor action in my legs and gave myself a reverse hug from behind.

Yoga can be rough in more ways than one.

The class was a challenging and humbling ride, especially when we lifted ourselves off the mat from various seated positions. Getting up off the ground was difficult. I had thought there was more strength in my core than what showed up!

But even more humbling were those tears. I had thought I was stronger in that regard, too.

Afterward, I simply concluded that my body is sometimes more conscious than my mind, and that it's okay to feel unbalanced when working to find my center.

And if a few uncertain tears pop up along the way, then that's okay, too.

Truth 5

Patience can be developed
when the mind is quieted.

Foundations

May you have a strong foundation when the winds of changes shift.

~FOREVER YOUNG, BOB DYLAN

I've been taking Rocket yoga for more than a year now.

Three times a week, I go to the same class with the same instructor. She mixes it up, and we fly and invert and lock and lift. I rarely miss a class, so I figure I've practiced Rocket more than 100 times.

How is it, then, that I've only recently realized that at every practice we move through a foundational sequence before we take off?

Am I the only one who didn't know we were putting on the undergarments of our practice before getting dressed for the rest?

Like most young girls, I was taught my first foundational lesson at an early age: *always wear nice underwear in case I'm in an accident and wind up in the hospital.*

Foundations can last a lifetime, and that's why, every day, I've got on pretty underwear, under there. And I think that's also why we are working on a foundation at Rocket. It's not just for that day's practice, but for the rest of our practicing days.

How is it that I am just catching on to this?

We do each pose for five breaths in a particular order, building one on the other, each new posture getting another five breaths and only adding the whistles and bells after completing both sides.

Maybe it's taken me this long to realize what's going on at the beginning because I'm so busy focusing on the middle. I'm waiting for what I think are the fun parts, like the handstands and the arm balances and the rest.

But here, at Rocket, and seemingly unbeknownst to me until now, we've apparently been threading together the foundation of a practice with patience and persistence.

It's almost as if the practice is one long home economics project, with the instructor the head seamstress, putting down the pattern and laying out the big pieces first, teaching us to stitch together the larger parts before adding on the beautiful buttons, the fancy pockets, the sparkling sequins.

It's methodical. It's challenging. And as with the creation of any lasting foundation, I think it's making me stronger.

I remember being in a sewing class in high school, and let's just say it wasn't a place where I excelled. There really was never any kind of foundation laid out in the class, nothing to build upon. We were just given a pattern and sent out to sea without a captain. I gave a shirt and a skirt my best efforts.

The instructor would walk around, looking down on those of us seated and sewing. Those around me seemed to do fine, but I'd be adrift, jamming the machine and ripping out the seams I'd just sewn. My mother rescued me, finishing my projects on the sly at home.

There is a foundation very specific to Ashtanga, the instructor says each time. *We'll do each pose, and when we add a new one, we'll hold it for five breaths. Then we'll add the binds and the balances.*

Maybe she announced this on *Day One,* I'm not sure. But it seems that for several days a week and for most weeks this year, I've been getting dressed layer by layer without knowing it.

It's only now that I see there's even been a pattern every week at every practice, each pose like a piece of fabric, each movement the placement of the pieces, with all the effort and sweat securing the seams in place.

We thread together the Sun A's and Sun B's and the Warrior I's and II's. We reach into Triangles and Reverse Triangles and Extended Side Angles, and seamlessly move into High Lunges and Reverse Extended Side Angles. We make sure the right and left sides match by repeating the same sequences on each.

And when we have completed this basic foundation, we reinforce its stitching, moving through it again, this time adding the trappings like Bound Half Moon, Bird of Paradise, Reverse Bird and more.

The other night, the practice room was packed, and it was hot. The instructor climbed up on the windowsill and braced herself inside its frame, looking down on us like Spiderman.

Think of me up here as your captain, so I can help guide you! she exclaimed. *Let's double dip,* she announced, referring to our yoga push-ups. *Be honest. This is your chance to get stronger!*

This all struck me as perfectly normal, with her in the window as captain and me at sea among the other yogis.

I'm here to build my foundation, so I listen to the captain and double dip as best I can. And I think it's working. My dips are feeling stronger.

Of course, it could just be the new underwear I bought to practice yoga. A fellow yogi had pointed them out in the store.

I picked up a pair and said, *If you see me flying in class, you'll know they're working.*

After that, I returned to buy some more. And of course I got some pretty colors, because any foundation is worth maintaining, especially if it helps me fly.

Sky Watcher

Blue days, all of them gone. Nothing but blue skies from now on.

~BLUE SKIES, WILLIE NELSON

One Sunday morning, I attended a yoga class in a new timeslot, and I saw the sky for the first time in Half Moon.

I have always been a sky watcher. Really, not a day goes by when I don't look up and note the sky. I love clear blue skies, dark and dangerous skies, and white cloudy skies. I especially like the night sky and have always stopped to look up at the stars. I have watched the constellations appear on one end of the sky and later in the night make their way to the other end.

And the moon! My favorite! On fall nights when there is a Harvest moon, or on winter nights when the Crescent moon comes close to Venus, it is standard operating procedure for me to text my children who live a few hundred miles away and ask, *See the moon?*

On this particular Sunday, I found myself off schedule and available for yoga at an unusual time. I left the house quickly, not even signing up for the class which had already begun by the time I arrived.

I grabbed my mat and placed it down in a corner. The room was hushed, the music was soft and everyone was holding a pose. I quietly joined in.

This class was listed as All Levels; however, it seemed to lean more toward an introductory class. The instructor described every move, demonstrated some basic poses and took us into the binds in baby steps.

A week or so earlier, I had been asking about how to advance my practice.

How am I supposed to get better? I had asked, wanting to know my yoga plan. *Do people just take years of classes and get better like that?*

My practice felt stuck. I missed what it felt like in the beginning, the excitement of learning and attempting a pose and finally accomplishing it. Everything was new to me then.

For you, I was told, *it would be about the energetics, and we will practice that today.*

I had no idea what energetics were but, during the class that followed this discussion, the instruction was incremental, leading us through the flows bit by bit.

In Warrior II, we were told to feel the energy up the front leg beginning at the big toe. We were asked to feel the outside edge of the back foot and note the energy running up that leg to meet the other. There was talk about Mula Bandha and lifting the pelvic floor. In Pyramid pose, we were instructed on where to place our right hip, our left hip, our sacrum. We were asked to feel the scissor action in our legs.

That day, my practice took on another dimension. I took note of the little movements as well as the big ones, and my body was more engaged than ever.

I was surprised to again find my practice deepening on this subsequent Sunday, when I showed up at an odd time and found myself in a quiet corner of a more entry level class. This class was all about the energetics, too. I was challenged by the more deliberate movements in each pose, and I eagerly absorbed the instructions on how to build and hold the poses.

And it was through these slow and considered motions that I was able to find the stability and strength that had to date eluded me in Half Moon. For the first time, instead of looking down or sideways while holding the pose, this sky watcher was finally able to lift her eyes upward.

During that Sunday morning yoga practice, looking up seemed to take every single muscle from my toes to my fingers and throughout my core. This was a major event for me in that quiet corner. It was as if going back to the beginning had brought me further along.

I wondered if maybe these energetics, or baby steps, had always been outlined, but that I had perhaps been remiss in tending to them. I'm often guilty of having too many ants in my pants during my practice.

This time, though, there were no ants marching. Slowing down invited a deeper practice and helped me find the sky.

Into the Heart

Take it easy, take it easy. Don't let the sound of your own wheels make you crazy.

~TAKE IT EASY, EAGLES

I pulled a double at yoga and found myself in an evening class, even though I had practiced that same morning.

I arrive with my mind busy from the day, and it feels good to enter the hot room, pin back my hair and lay out my mat. Everything about entering the room and setting up helps me to step out of the day and into the moment. It is a quick and welcome transition.

And there is so much breathing.

In yoga, we practice on our breath, and every move is associated with an inhale or an exhale.

I used to be antsy with the breathing. Having to breathe slowly and intentionally does not always come easily. I am high functioning. I'm a multi-tasker. Taking things slowly and breathing deeply has to be intentional for me because it's not exactly in my nature.

We start on the floor with a simple twist. And we breathe. We make our way to the opposite side. And we breathe.

We stand and reach to the heavens on an inhale, pushing our hearts upward. And we fold to the floor on an exhale, dropping our heads. We inhale to lift halfway and exhale to fold once more.

On and on, we move, and we breathe.

Your breath connects you to your practice, the instructor says. *It takes you out of your mind and into your heart where you can live through being and feeling, not thinking.*

I have always had a busy mind.

I remember reviewing the day when I was little, as I lay in bed before sleep. I would make up stories, changing events of the day if I wished they had gone differently. Even now, as an adult, my mind can be reviewing the day when my brain should be shutting off for sleep.

And, in general, I have always struggled with overthinking that which doesn't sit well with me. Stillness can elude me, in both body and mind. I have even tried to learn how to meditate, but I can't even seem to reach the beginner's five minutes of quiet.

We bring our hands to our hearts and say three Oms aloud. And we're told to touch our hearts with our thumbs while our hands are in prayer as a reminder to connect to the heart.

I touch my thumbs to my heart with my mind still busy checking off events of the day. One Om and I'm reviewing the logistics of a work event. Another Om and I'm thinking about a friend. One last Om and I'm thinking my most important thought: what I plan to eat for dinner!

We exhale to another forward fold and inhale to a flat back before transitioning through our first vinyasa.

In one long exhale, I place my hands down and step back into Plank, hovering above the mat before releasing into a low push-up. I inhale as I straighten my arms and drop my hips, pulling my heart forward into an Upward Facing Dog. Then, I exhale back into my inverted V, or Downward Facing Dog.

We rest there in Down Dog for three more breaths, and my mind finally begins to settle. This evening's practice seems to be the slowest I've ever done and, most likely, the most intentional.

Through the breathing, I seem to be able to concentrate more on the poses and less on my thoughts. And each time we lift our hearts, the instructor emphasizes the inhale, telling us to push our hearts forward to feel it.

Life is lived when we are feeling, not when we are doing, the instructor says.

I inhale and exhale and connect to the practice and to what she is saying. And there, in the yoga studio, I am finally out of my mind and into my heart.

Power

*Carry on, my wayward son, for there'll be peace when you are done. Lay your
weary head to rest.*

--WAYWARD SON, KANSAS

I used to practice in front of mirrors.

I liked it. It reminded me of my long ago dance classes. And it gave me a larger sense of the room, because I could look forward and still see behind me.

But for a while now, I've been practicing without the mirrors. At first, it was a little unsettling. At one studio, I found myself looking into the eyes of those facing me. At another, I found myself staring at a wall. At still another, I found myself looking out a window onto the busy city streets.

After a while, though, the weirdness went away.

Now it's not so freaky to look someone in the eye across the room. And the cracks and the slats in the walls and windows serve as my stare points to help me find my balance. The city streets outside the windows are no longer a distraction, and I've even watched the rain fly sideways across the floor-to-ceiling windows, as I've flowed inside while it's thundered outside.

I don't miss the mirrors now and no longer need to look forward to see what's behind me.

So now the image of my practice is mostly in my mind, which is sometimes a tumultuous place. Sometimes the person in there is tough when the practice is rough and wonders why I'm not stronger or more flexible, why I can't catch the balance or catch more air.

And so it was with wonder that I viewed a video of one of my instructor's classes. There's a beautiful soundtrack, and I can't hear anything that was going on in my mind. The video is a mirror of the practice, and all I see in its reflection is the power and grace of everyone in it.

The video translates the almost tangible power of flow. Watching it, I can feel the strength captured in the movements, the flexibility found in the folds and the bravery beneath the balances.

It was a beautiful practice that provided both power and peace.

The other night, in yet another practice, we were in Rag Doll. Our heads hung heavy between our cradled arms as we folded in half.

Put your head down, the instructor said to the man behind me. He placed his hand on the man's head and asked, *Do you think a lot?*

Yes, I do, the man answered, honesty spilling forth from his fold.

Well, I think I'm someone who's been blessed not to think too much, the instructor said. *It's okay to rest your head and just not think.*

And so it goes for me with the practice and the flow. It's what lets me find my strength while resting my head. It's always there, the power and the peace.

And now I can even watch it on video.

Obsession

We're captive on the carousel of time. We can't return, we can only look behind from where we came, and go round and round and round in the circle game.

~CIRCLE GAME, JONI MITCHELL

It's the first chilly Sunday morning of the fall, and I am anxious to attend the mid-morning yoga class.

This is one of my favorite classes. It is the perfect hour, still the morning but with time to laze around a bit. It is crowded, the people are all friendly, and the class lasts longer than usual. There is something about the large group and the extra time. From the start, the energy is high, and it's catching.

We move from pose to pose with the instructor taking us through many different sequences. We move from Yoga Squat to Crow to a vinyasa. We flow from Warrior I to Warrior II to Triangle Pose. We inhale and exhale with each movement, and it never crosses my mind to look at the clock on the wall.

Regardless, this clock has all its numbers in a heap at the bottom with a quote that reads, *Who cares?*

This particular weekend, my mind is at ease. It's a welcome relief as it had been busy, busy, busy in the brain. The past few weeks had been somewhat overwhelming, and it seemed that my mind was only resting when I slept. Even then, I'm not sure my sleep counted as rest as some of what I was busy with seemed to be appearing in my dreams!

We're going to move from one pose to another without thinking, the instructor says. *Don't overthink it. Just move into it. The body will know what to do if you don't think too hard.*

We pop down from standing into Yoga Squat, low to the ground with feet hip-width distance apart and hands in prayer at the heart. We move right into

Crow, tilting forward, hands on the mat, knees on the arms, and feet off the ground. We pop back up, lift the right knee, grab the ankle and move into Dancer, the body in a standing backbend.

We stand once more and reach to the sky, step the feet apart, and pop back down into Yoga Squat.

No time to think. No time to stop.

If you think too hard, it can stop you from what you are doing, the instructor continues as we continue the flow on the other side.

In the past, I have found myself in times where too much thinking has stopped me from what I am doing. It's like being on a roller coaster in the brain, and it is precious time lost, that is for certain. Always, when things settle down, I look back with wonder at how I could let myself hop on such a ride.

We stand in my favorite pose, Warrior II, legs stretched from front to back in a lunge, the back foot parallel to the back edge of the mat, the front foot perpendicular to the front edge of the mat, the hips and arms opened to the side.

Let's move into Half Moon with reckless abandon, the instructor announces.

Reckless abandon! I like those words!

I fling myself forward onto my front leg, lifting up the back leg and keeping my arms spread. I hover on one foot with one hand toward the mat and the other toward the sky, then step back to Warrior II and, again without thinking, back to Half Moon.

With reckless abandon, I repeat the sequence with the class three times.

Moving without thinking is actually very freeing. My body does what it needs to do because my mind is free.

At the end of class, I join the others in a quiet seat with my hands in prayer and my mind at ease. And as we inhale together, I have a reckless thought.

What if I never hopped on that roller coaster ride ever again?

And as we exhale together, I seal this new thought with what I hope is my most wild abandon.

Weightlessness

Can the child within my heart rise above? ... But time makes you bolder, even children get older.

~LANDSLIDE, STEVIE NICKS

I was pretty lucky to have enjoyed a fairly carefree childhood.

I have wonderful memories, especially of summer evenings when all my neighborhood friends would gather on the front lawn to play games, ride bikes and stay out until dark.

In my elementary school years, I was actually pretty adventurous. I'd hop on the back of my friend's bicycle, and he would drive wildly all over the streets, careening down the hills at top speed. We would do the same on his skateboard, riding double with me hanging on for dear life.

He tied a stick to a rope to a tree, and I hopped on and swung over the backyard creek from one bank to the other, until I had to jump off before getting stuck while still over the water.

I would ride my bike with no hands, fearless, and walk on the stilts my father made. I would grab the top of the garage while straddling a unicycle that belonged to the boy across the street, and pedal from one side of the driveway to the other. We even climbed inside a tire tube and rolled down the hill on the side of the house.

The front lawn was like a tumbling mat, and we would do somersaults, backbends, walkovers, handsprings and cartwheels until the stars came out.

These I consider the weightless times of my growing-up years.

I remember that expanded feeling inside my chest when it was time to play outside at the end of the day after dinner. My biggest concern was whether it was still light enough to stay outside.

I am pretty lucky to have enjoyed that weightless feeling again, and it happened in the yoga studio during the inversion segment of class.

As usual, we moved our mats to the wall. I placed both hands down in front of me, gearing up while trying to visualize myself in an upside down Mountain pose where the body is stretched tall and straight and strong.

Again and again, I attempted to lift myself into a handstand.

As before, I popped into several handstands, only to have one foot or the other tap the wall behind me as I played at the balance, trying to get both feet to stand on the ceiling.

I listened to the various directions the instructor called out and repeated the effort several times.

When it was finally time to bring our mats back to the center of the room, I figured I would give it one more try. Without any time to think, I kicked up easily and found the sweet spot, lingering upside down.

There was no pressure in my palms and no attempt to keep the balance. I was just simply and suddenly dangling there, upside down and weightless, and that expanded feeling in my chest from when I was nine years old came back as if it were yesterday.

It's been a while since this effort, and many more practices have followed. Still, finding a handstand with no thought at all seems to be an exercise in and of itself. Clearing my mind to what it must have been as a young child seems to be an integral part of my success. It sounds so simple; yet, as with the handstand itself, it remains an ongoing challenge.

Now my goal is to do my handstands in the middle of the room, away from the wall.

And this proves to be an even bigger challenge, as I have to not only clear my mind but also be as fearless as that little girl, swinging over the creek and zooming down the hill, feet off the bike pedals and hands in the air.

Truth 6

Courage can be discovered
when personal power is unlocked.

Fearlessness

It's time to try defying gravity. I think I'll defy gravity.

~DEFYING GRAVITY, WICKED

One summer, my daughter climbed more than 50 feet above the ground, strapped on a harness, grabbed a bar and jumped off a platform.

She flew on a flying trapeze next to the Hudson River!

Often, my daughter will call as she walks to various destinations on her errands in the city, and this day was no different. She was preparing her spring jewelry line, even though it was not yet fall. It had turned August into a hectic month as she designed and produced her pieces. She called to vent about the hitches and obstacles she was facing.

I am an understanding and patient mother.

I don't understand why all that is making you crazy! I exclaimed. *Why aren't you beside yourself about going on a flying trapeze?!? Call me when it's over!*

My daughter has always been what I call a participant. At five years old, she let the summer camp counselor put a floatie on her back, and she jumped off the high dive. She learned how to swim without hesitation. Growing up, she went on every roller coaster no matter how high or how many loops. She's been hot-air ballooning twice.

She is always game to try something new. And now the flying trapeze.

Are you sure she's your daughter? my friends ask me.

I am cautious. I was not always this way. As a young child, I was pretty much a tomboy. Growing up, I would just go along following my gut, not thinking too hard about much and making decisions easily.

In yoga, I've had to tap back into that fearlessness, wherever it hides, in order to attempt the many poses. When I first started practicing, I could get into some of the poses by virtue of simply being coordinated. But as I progressed, yoga seemed to demand more of me, and not just strength and stretch and balance.

It demanded fearlessness, and it started with Crow.

Crow begins with Yoga Squat. Crouched low on the mat, hands are placed in front of the feet with elbows bent. Knees sneak up onto the backs of the arms, climbing as high as they can. The body tilts forward, the hips lift up, and the feet come off the ground.

The instructor would demonstrate Crow for the room. He would easily lean into it and go even further, pressing into his hands and raising his body into the air, his legs lifting easily toward the sky, floating diagonally and against gravity on just his hands, his face clearing a space above the mat.

For myself, I feared a face plant.

Once you are not afraid to teeter forward, he'd say, *you will be able to feel it and find it.*

It took quite some time for me to risk the fear of leaning forward and to trust enough to find that teeter point. It was scary and counterintuitive. However, after a while, it made sense to my body, even if not to my mind, and I found it.

Today, I move easily into Crow. I straighten my arms and dome my upper back, and I lift myself up and away from the mat.

Perched there, it is a far cry from climbing 50 feet in the air and flying above a net but, to me, I am soaring.

A Child

I'm still standing better than I ever did, looking like a true survivor, feeling like a little kid.

~I'M STILL STANDING, ELTON JOHN

Am I supposed to heed a message when I hear the same thing more than once from unrelated sources?

I am thinking so, even if it's a message I don't want to hear. The message is that, in many respects, I am like a child.

At midlife, how can this be?

When I first started yoga, the poses really clicked with childhood memories of tumbling on my front lawn with neighborhood kids, of gym classes in elementary school, of good times when I was little with no cares and no fears.

As a child, I was all over the trampoline. I could do walkovers and backbends. I cartwheeled and somersaulted all over the front yard.

And now, I am grown. *A responsible adult* as my adult nephew teases me, laughing at what he considers ironic. To him, I'm an overgrown kid! He doesn't think like I did when I was little, that once you were an adult, you were all grown up. That was an endpoint in my young mind.

As an adult, I would not have guessed that I would be doing handstands and yoga what-not at my age, much less looking forward to it and doing it all week long, having never before really exercised.

In that way, I do feel like a child, and that's a good feeling.

So when someone I look to for wise advice told me that he sees me almost like a child, I was a little surprised.

I have raised my children on my own, handled my finances, bought a house and a car, found a job and generally made lots and lots of what I consider grown-up decisions over the years.

He was, however, referring to another type of growing up. He was talking about growing into my whole self, not looking to others for validation and growing into what he calls my own power as a woman.

This gave me pause, because I never see myself as challenged in this way, and it made me think of a quote that I've many times made sure to impress upon my children:

> *Our deepest fear is not that we are inadequate. Our deepest fear is*
> *that we are powerful beyond measure.*
>
> ~Marianne Williamson

I am not supposed to be afraid of myself!

Within a week of this discussion, I have my annual physical, and I'm told that my lab results are so clean and healthy, they look like those of a child.

You don't drink, you don't smoke, and you don't have any fun! the doctor joked.

A joke to him, but real to me. I have lived a quiet life for some time now. Most likely, I have not realized my potential power. Unfaced fears can act as a fortress and, apparently, I've launched my children but not myself.

Within a few days, I am back in the yoga studio. We are in Utkatasana, or Chair pose. I am standing with my legs and feet squeezed tightly together, knees bent and hips dipped low. My heart lifts and my arms spark upward alongside my ears.

This is a pose we do several times in every practice. It is nothing new.

This is a familiar pose, the instructor says. *But today I want it to be brand new to you. I want you to experience it like a child.*

I sit in my imaginary chair like a child. It is a difficult pose, but this grown-up yogi makes her best effort to find comfort in her seat, even so.

Overboard

Ground she's movin' under me. Tidal waves out on the sea.

~VOLCANO, JIMMY BUFFET

I went overboard in the yoga studio.

Faced a fear and lived to tell!

I consider my yoga mat a safe haven. Like a kindergartner who pulls out a mat during rest period, I am content to arrive at yoga, unroll my mat, step onto it and claim my space.

My mat is longer than my body and less than a yard wide. My first two were purple, my favorite color since my kindergarten days, and the one I use now is blue, a close second.

The yoga practice takes place one hundred percent on the mat. One yogi, one mat. Some classes can be so crowded that I'm only inches from my neighbor, but there's an unspoken code that each mat honors a personal space.

The yoga mat is home to every student and to every asana.

Asana is a Sanskrit word that has evolved to mean *posture* or *pose*, but its original meaning is *seat*, referring to a position held at length in meditation. Today, though, this word has come to mean so much more.

It is more than a position, more than a stretch, more than a balance. Each asana works to open the body's energy channels, soothing not just physical maladies, but mental and spiritual ones, too.

There are lots of asanas for this kind of work. There are standing ones like Chair and Eagle and Dancer. There are those that exercise the core like Crow and Boat. There are even restorative ones, including everybody's favorite, Child's pose.

The one in which I went overboard is the handstand. This should be no surprise. Months earlier, I had set a new goal for myself: a handstand in the middle of the room.

Usually, I'd only practice this asana near the wall which would serve as my security blanket should I begin to fall into a backbend while upside down. If I'd begin to tilt, I'd just tap my toes on the wall in an effort to realign myself and find my balance.

To try for this asana mid-room, there is a part of the flow sequence where, instead of remaining in Standing Split, the foot on the ground can press down to go up in an effort to achieve a handstand.

It was several months into my efforts of trying to pop up during this sequence before I experienced a fluke and found myself upside down in the pose, mid-room. After that, I tried as best I could to recapture the balance and do it again, but weeks and weeks followed, and I found myself almost giving up by playing it safe in Standing Split.

Then there came the day I decided to give it another go. I cleared my mind, placed my hands on the mat, lifted my right leg and then pushed off with my left. And safe on my mat but without the security of the wall, I inverted my body for at least a nanosecond.

Mid-room! It was brief, but I was there! I got so excited that I popped right out of it and immediately stood upright.

It was over fast, but it had delivered enough confidence to stay with me until the next time. And that next time turned out to be a few days later.

I arrived at class equipped with the remnants of confidence from the previous practice, some coffee under my belt and a good night's sleep. When it came time to give it a go, I kicked right up. Then what followed seemed to transpire pretty much in slow motion. I would say I found the balance, inverted in a handstand, mid-room; but, really, I don't think that was the case. I had what seemed like an endless internal discussion while upside down.

I'm up! I think I'm balanced. Maybe not? I don't think so! How long have I lasted? Am I bending backward?

In reality, probably no more than a split second had passed before my legs tipped over backward, my body followed, and I called out, unabashedly, *OVERBOARD!*

My feet absorbed most of the fall before my head followed and the rest of me landed with a splat on the ground.

Not pretty!

I turned onto my stomach and hugged my mat like a lifeboat while answering my fellow yogis' concerns that I was okay, declaring that I might need another month before mustering up the courage to try this asana again.

With that, I collected myself and rejoined the rest of the practice.

Safe on my mat once more, I realized I was no worse for wear. And as I started to flow, I even had the fleeting thought that a month might be way too long to wait before I set sail again.

Adventure

So come out of your cave walking on your hands and see the world hanging upside down.

~THE CAVE, MUMFORD AND SONS

The other night, I was at yoga, laying out my mat, unwinding it from its bag and doing the same from my day.

I prefer a spot against the wall, where I can try a few handstands without going overboard.

I walk along my mat and talk with those nearby, enjoying the switch from my workday to my yoga night, chatting and pacing and popping into handstands.

And I wonder where else, really, would this seem normal?

Aside from my Instagram friend who sneaks photos in her office attire, putting up pictures of handstands alongside a file cabinet or backbends atop a conference table, I'm not sure I know anywhere else I could chat while upside down without anyone wondering what's wrong with me.

I've come to realize that I feel the most like myself when I'm at yoga. It's nice here, more than nice. There is a freedom once I park my car and walk to the studio, as if I am leaving one life and showing up at another.

And this transition has been a huge adventure for someone like me, someone who doesn't love change and who takes comfort in sameness.

It's not that I'm not who I am outside of yoga. It's pretty hard to be anyone else, anyway. It's just that on my mat I feel the closest to me and to the girl I was so long ago.

On my mat, *it just is what it is*, a phrase I usually hate to hear. It's the phrase I come up against when no amount of justifying or explaining can make things how

I'd rather they be. It's the phrase that speaks the truth, and that's what I get on my mat.

It is what it is on the mat because it's pretty bare there, and so am I. Even what I wear is bare, my shoulders, sometimes my midriff and even my feet. Once there, I put up my hair, which for me is a fairly personal thing. Off the mat and outside the house, my hair is always down and done.

The yogi seated to my right looks up at me as if we'd been in conversation and exclaims, *Wouldn't that be amazing?*

What? I ask, realizing that she thinks I've overheard the yogi on her other side.

To have the kind of job that can take you anywhere? she answers. *Where you get to go anywhere?*

No! I say immediately back. *I'm a homebody,* I admit from my mat, coming down from a handstand against the comfort of the wall. *I don't want to go all over the place! Coming here is my big adventure!*

But then I sit down to ask this young girl where her job takes her and find that she has just returned from several months in Australia, studying dolphins. And from my perch on my mat, I am indeed amazed.

My yogi friends are big adventurers. To me, it seems they are afraid of nothing. I love to hear where they've been and what they've done. They are young and brave and adventurous, and I am doing my best to learn from them.

I am on the road back from something, an adventure that had been chaotic and challenging. I had been young and brave and adventurous then, and I think that's what helped me through at the time. It's just that I thought the objective was to find peace and safety, kind of like the spot against the wall where I can't fall over if I go upside down.

The classes I take are pretty powerful, and maybe that's why I've met so many adventurous people, those that run and bike and ski and more, those that aren't necessarily looking for peace or safety. And when I wonder what I'm doing here among them, I think back to when I was young and brave and adventurous, too.

Maybe I am trying to find that girl again.

One yogi friend runs to yoga, takes the class and runs home. She did this throughout her pregnancy, all the while being one of the few who could hold the backbends for the full counts. Another yogi is an avid skier who just spent a recent afternoon on a trampoline. And there's the man who completed 20 years in the military who hopes to teach as part of Yoga for Wounded Warriors.

My son's a yogi, and he's jumped out of an airplane. Yet another yogi biked to the beach, more than 100 miles away, as part of a fundraising event. Still another friend hails from across the globe, having spent more than a year teaching yoga in the States only to return to her country for yet another brave beginning.

And how can I not mention the young woman who spent many years as a platform diver, studied in faraway places, and is recovering from a knee injury received while cliff diving. She is forever my example of grace and strength and determination as she maintains her practice, her work, and her indomitable spirit while healing.

The night's practice is intense, and I am glad to reach the end when it's time for inversions. As before, I pop into a handstand, secured by the wall behind me. After balancing a bit, I lower my legs and stand up for a breather. I face the wall, thinking how much I like this part of the practice, with the room dark, the music playing and everyone upside down.

A tap on my shoulder catches me by surprise, and someone's hands spin me out of my reverie. It's the instructor, turning me to face front, away from the wall.

It's just so seamless at this point, she says. *No more wall for you. Hope you don't mind and hope you had fun there, because you're done with that.*

She stands there and, under unspoken instructions, I place my palms on the mat and lift my legs into a handstand away from the wall. Each time I wobble, I feel the instructor point my core back to where it should be, so I can be upside down but still stable.

And just like that, I am set on a course for a new adventure, joining the ranks of those around me and getting that much closer to the girl who had been there once before.

Catch Me!

Upside down. Who's to say what's impossible and can't be found?

~UPSIDE DOWN, JACK JOHNSON

I was in a very hot yoga practice, and we were more than halfway through. The day had only half-begun, I was only half-caffeinated, and we were in Eagle pose.

For some reason, I've been having trouble keeping my balance in Eagle. I try to find a point in front of me to clear my mind, so I don't even have to think about balancing, but that only makes me think about it all the more, and over I go.

This day in Eagle, my mind is already moving quickly ahead. Usually, we do Eagle on both sides, right and then left, and then right and then left again. Sometimes, after the second time around, we move into bound Warrior III and then into Standing Split.

And then I know what's coming next. In fact, my mind is already there while I am wrapping myself up in Eagle. At this point, those of us who want to pop into a handstand get to give it a try.

Before practice, I usually attempt a few handstands. I've been working on these forever, and now I'm working on them without the wall. And I can never tell when they're going to show up.

At best, they've been sporadic guests. They arrived the summer before but then left the following fall. They were home for the holidays but then disappeared again. And ever since, I've been doing my best to get them to return for good.

And they hate the heat. It's especially tough to find them in a hot practice.

I'm a fairly visual person, and usually I have to see things to put them to memory. In general, I think this is just how I learn and process most things. I've been doodling since I was little, from pictures in my mind to pictures on the page.

So now, to achieve my handstand, I find myself using lots of visualization.

Sometimes I picture myself being pulled in and up, as I was when upside down in a handstand workshop. Balancing there, I saw two feet step under my nose before two hands wrapped themselves around my lower belly and pressed.

This assist automatically lifted and straightened me beyond where I was. And once I was upright and saw it was the instructor, I told him that not only was I surprised not to have recognized his feet that I'd been watching for the better part of an hour, but that I couldn't believe I had any room left for any more lift.

It also helps to picture my friend who emailed from her vacation about the freedom she felt when practicing handstands on a yoga deck. She said the outside space freed her mind, allowing her body to easily achieve the pose.

And since then, on my way upside down, I visualize lots of space all around and even more above, and I imagine my feet reaching upward beyond the ceiling toward that vacation sky and into its clouds, and this seems to help my whole body follow.

I also picture my shoulder girdle, which I used to think was between my shoulders and across my back but now actually realize surrounds each shoulder. Going up, I picture my shoulders encased in something strong, so they can stack above my wrists and provide a sturdy base for my torso.

So, really, there is an entire artist's rendering going on in my mind when I invert and sometimes even long before.

This day, the paintbrushes start flying in Eagle. And when it comes time to try a few handstands, my palette is already prepared.

I hop up on my good side. My right leg in the air, I push off lightly with my left and picture my hips stacking, waiting for the feeling that lets me know I have it, that lets me know it's okay for my left leg to meet my right.

And, slowly, I make the connection, upside down.

But that lightness, that stillness, that space where I pull in my belly for my feet to reach the clouds, eludes me, and I feel my feet start to draw outside the lines, moving farther over my hips to the wrong side of the room.

And in this quiet and hot room, where the only sound is the breath, I distinguish myself without warning, calling out the instructor's name followed by a plea:

CATCH ME!

But I never feel his catch because, somehow, I catch myself. Somehow, and I don't know how, I get myself straightened out.

It seems my panic cleared my mind, so my body could do its work. The instructor later tells me I did it by grabbing the floor with my fingertips and pulling in my core. I had no idea. I couldn't picture it!

All I know is that the preparation that started in Eagle that day blocked my view, making it difficult for me to see the whole picture. And in the end, I was somehow able to save myself on instinct.

This instructor impresses on the class to let go of our stories when we arrive on the mat. We are not supposed to predetermine the practice. We're just supposed to *be,* and we do this through the breath.

But this day it takes my panic to make me present, which isn't exactly the game plan. Even so, learning that I can save myself when I think I need someone to catch me isn't too bad a takeaway.

Still, I'm leaving the light on for those handstands.

It's as if they're not mine, I told this same instructor, days earlier. *It's as if each time I'm wondering if they're going to show up.*

Maybe my mental artwork is more on display than I think, because he just looked at me with a smile and, without words, pointed to his head, making the perfect picture for the next time I go upside down.

My Spot

I have a favorite spot in each of my yoga classes.

At one studio, I like to set up on the left in the front row. At another, I like to be in the middle of the back row. At yet another, I like to line up my mat in front of one of the many windows.

I wonder what I would do if the instructors insisted on our choosing different spots each time? As a yogi, I hear so much talk about moving in new directions. And while I think I'm doing my best to evolve and transform, I know my tendency is just to find what's comfortable and set up shop.

The other night I was late, and someone was in *my spot*. So I placed my mat a few spaces to his right. But that put me front and center, which I didn't want, and so I got up and placed my mat to his left in the space right next to him.

Hope you don't mind if I go here. I said, as if my indecision needed an excuse.

But the room wasn't as full as usual, and it felt silly to be an inch away from my neighbor with so many open spaces. So I got up and moved yet again.

Outside my usual spot, I felt a little out of place! And then the instructor talked about leaving our cocoons where things are familiar and safe.

Get out of the nest, he said. *You may find comfort in there, but it's boring in the nest!*

When I am sweating and flowing and doing the poses, these words make so much sense.

Of course! I think to myself, standing on one leg and lifting the other out and back behind me in Dancer pose. *I'm ready for lots of new things!* I think to myself while all wrapped up in Eagle pose.

I decide this spot is not so bad after all, and I'm a bird who's already left the nest by the time we hit the floor. The standing part of the practice is over. We get a chance to catch our breath as we lie on our stomachs for a moment's rest. And I'm amazed at how quickly I pull back into myself. I know what's coming next. It's the part I don't like. Backbends like Locust and Bow with our hips on the floor. And then more backbends like Camel and Wheel with our hips off the floor.

I like the standing part of the practice. I dance right through the Warrior I's and II's, through the binds and the balances, through the Triangle poses and their reversals. This is what comes naturally to me. This is what feels familiar. This is what I find most comfortable.

For me, the seated part of the practice is the hard part. It's like trying to find a spot when mine is already taken. I can't quite find my groove. It's a challenge to straighten my arms in the backbends. It's a challenge to reach the ground in the splits. And don't even get me started on seated straddle, a pose for which I don't think my body was really made.

By this time, I'm thinking I want my spot back!

But it's kind of an illusion to think there is only ever one spot for one person. And I realize now that for all the many new starts I've had, for all the new spots I've found, there will always be the need to seek out more.

When I was a little girl, I thought you just grew up, and that was that. Even as a young adult, I still held on to that belief. Only now am I realizing that we are always leaving the nest. It's a continual process.

We do some abdominal work and an inversion, and then we move into the resting pose of Pigeon. Lately, I've gotten pretty good at not fidgeting in Pigeon, but on this night, the instructor takes to talking about the task of making ourselves vulnerable in order to make connections.

For me, this is worse than any floor work, worse than any Wheel, Camel, Bow or Lizard.

And that's because I know that doing so is the only way to leave the nest and find the next spot that's right for me.

Truth 7

Inner power can be realized
when perseverance is achieved.

Exit Strategy

I want to fly like an eagle to the sea. Fly like an eagle, let my spirit carry me.

~FLY LIKE AN EAGLE, STEVE MILLER BAND

Life pretty much cooks along for the most part.

In general, things go according to plan in what my son refers to as *The Land of Anne.*

Sometimes, though, challenges pop up along several fronts, and I can find myself navigating some choppy waters. Sometimes, it can feel as if I have been at sea for a while.

And that's when I'm most eager to attend a yoga class, hoping to find calm with the room baking, the sweat dripping, the muscles working and the instructor talking.

Stay in it, she says. *It was your decision to come here. Don't think about running now.*

We are in Eagle pose with Garudasana arms and Garudasana legs.

This pose begins in Chair, with legs and feet pressed tightly together, knees bent like a skier, arms extended and the heart lifted. The right leg lifts off the ground and wraps over the left at the knee, while the right arm wraps under and around the other at the elbow. The eyes find their focal point, or drishti, and the body holds the pose.

In this class, we face the windows. I hold the pose, trying to keep my balance while standing on one foot with the rest of me wrapped up tightly.

The instructor continues her wise words.

Some of you might be thinking about your exit strategy right now. Maybe you think you can't do the pose like the others, that you are different and that is reason enough to leave. Maybe you difference yourself out in life, too. That is how we isolate ourselves.

I hover in Eagle pose, my muscles protesting. Am I more open to listening when my body is working its hardest? I blink the sweat into my eyes, and it occurs to me that, at times, I've used what I perceive as my differences from others to take flight from situations. It's an easy way to opt out of conflict, a quick and easy escape.

I think then about a complicated confluence of events and, while the instructor speaks, I imagine myself unlocking the window that serves as my drishti, spreading my wings like the eagle I am at the moment and flying away.

But that would be too easy, even if it were possible.

We switch sides, first reaching to the heavens before settling down again and, this time, wrapping the left leg over and the left arm under. I look out the window, find my drishti once more, and listen as the instructor encourages us to maintain the pose.

It's when things get difficult that the good stuff happens, she says. *Stay in the pose. You did not decide to be here just for the easy parts.*

An eagle can learn a lot, and this made sudden sense to me. Ordinarily, I'd want to take a detour from my challenges; however, I know that life is not made up of only the easy parts. Life gets complicated. It gets messy. Not everything can always be fine in the *Land of Anne.*

Just the other day, I had been discussing with a colleague some of the challenges I found myself facing. It was unusual for me to chat much along these lines as I mostly keep my own counsel. But it was raining, there was coffee and the office was cozy. It was conducive to a chat.

You are entering a new season, my colleague told me. *A blessing is coming your way.*

Turns out, her mother always tells her that when things get rough in all directions, big changes are coming. Surprisingly, these words made me feel instantly better. I could be ready for a new season! I could be ready for a blessing!

Both sides complete, we unwrap our Eagle arms and legs and stand tall as we stretch to the heavens once more before bringing our hands to rest at heart center.

Relief. Release. The hard part is over. I had stayed in it and was better for it.

Suck It Up!

Teach me. I know I'm not a hopeless case.

~BEAUTIFUL DAY, U2

It seems like forever since I've been working on my handstands.

In every single class, I am upside down and trying to remain so. If I happen to be at a class where none are done, I stay after so I can work on a few of my own.

At one time, I was in a class where we were working on a straddle handstand. Pressing down on my mat, I moved my feet as close to my hands as possible. In my mind's eye, I pressed down to go up. I wanted to pull in my belly and straddle my feet while raising them up to land a handstand.

This type of press handstand was new to me, and I was visualizing what I had seen on YouTube.

Everyone was helping each other, and one incredible yogi did a demonstration on a neighboring mat. She even gave me some pointers, like pushing my ponytail against the wall while upside down before lifting my feet. I could push my ponytail alright, but the effort only resulted in a few, funny-looking bunny hops.

A week later, it was my second at bat, and I was once again in my starting position, a very, very short Down Dog with my ponytail against the wall. I readied myself before trying to hoist my feet into a straddle handstand.

Hippity hop, once. My feet popped up a bit. Hippity hop, twice. They lifted a bit more. A few more hops, and I got my feet to the point where I felt a momentary hang, but not one that counted for much.

The yogi beside me was jumping into her handstand. She was all over it and very inspiring. But I returned to my regular version, pretending there was no wall standing guard. I landed it a few times and measured my success by the number of toe prints left behind.

That day, there was more handstand news, and it was some advice for the handstand vinyasa. The instructions were to lift lightly off the mat. No jumping. No scissor kick. No pop. We were told to engage more in the core to find it.

This might sound silly but, for me, it was all very exciting. Anything challenging is a yoga gift, and I am eager to open such new presents.

Could I find some inner meaning in all of this? Nope. Not yet. The only inner anything I could figure was to engage more of my core for success in these handstands.

Suck it up! advised a fellow yogi as I looked down at my hands pressed to the mat with my feet inched up close.

Mula Bandha and Uddiyana Bandha! she called out.

Bandhas are locks, and she was telling me to lock my pelvic floor (Mula Bandha) and my abdomen (Uddiyana Bandha) before lifting off the ground.

I locked in everything and hoisted myself up with a holler of triumph! It worked!

See? Mula Bandha and Uddiyana Bandha, my fellow yogi repeated.

I found more meaning in her earlier words.

Suck it up!

Sometimes, it's just what you have to do in order to get where you want to go.

Cinderella

Looking back we've touched on sorrowful days. Future pass, they disappear. You
will find peace of mind, if you look way down in your heart and soul.

~THAT'S THE WAY OF THE WORLD, EARTH, WIND & FIRE

Once upon a time, I believed in only good things.

I just assumed that I could anticipate what might be coming next, that it would be positive, and that things, whatever they might be, would simply just fall into place. It's a fair assumption that I grew up pretty much believing I would lead the life of Cinderella. Prince Charming and all.

The first segment of my yoga class is usually a standard flow. So for the first part of the practice, I can usually anticipate what might be coming next. We reach high and tilt back. We fold over and bow low. We lift halfway and straighten our backs, and we fold again with hands to the mat. We flow through our vinyasa, doing our best to float into a low push-up, through to an Upward Facing Dog, and back to a Downward Facing Dog.

And we step forward and do it again. I breathe, and it comes easily.

And then the practice really begins. We move into challenging poses, and I don't always know what's next. Some days it comes easily, and some days it does not. Regardless, it's always work to get through it.

Set your gaze, the instructor says as he chastises the class for looking around the room. *That's how you find your balance.*

As a Cinderella in the making, I basically breezed through the first segment of my life. Growing up, I had a nurturing family, learning came easily, and so did making friends. I excelled at my endeavors, whether it was my studies or dancing or drawing, and my college graduation found me standing in front of my graduating class as speaker and valedictorian. A wedding followed, and we settled into a home with two beautiful children and our wonderful dog.

Cinderella had arrived. This was my life's first segment, my standard flow. I had anticipated it all, and it had come easily.

But, as with the practice itself, what followed the initial flow were so many unanticipated challenges. This Cinderella tried as best she could to look ahead and set her gaze but could not always find her balance.

We twist our bodies into Eagle pose, standing on one foot and wrapping up our legs at the knees and interlacing our arms at the elbows. We are encouraged to set our gaze for balance and to not resist the difficulty of the pose.

Still twisted and on one foot, I curl into as small a ball as possible.

When it gets hard, that's when you breathe, the instructor says.

So maybe I was not really Cinderella. She had her challenges first and then lived happily ever after. My challenges came later. The marriage, the home, the dog - all gone. My assumptions and expectations - challenged. My flow - interrupted. On my own with my two beautiful children, I had no choice but to set my gaze and find my balance. So that's what I did for the years that followed.

Today my children are grown, and I have the gift of watching them support themselves and each other.

I unwind from Eagle pose, untangling my arms and legs, standing tall and reaching toward the sky. It is such a satisfying stretch, to reach up high like this after standing on one leg while all curled up for so long.

After so many years, I have had an epiphany of sorts. Looking back, I'm surprised to realize that I had effectively twisted myself into as small a ball as possible, unknowingly protecting myself from my life's flow. It has been a challenge to unwind, but I am learning to breathe in the face of challenge rather than resist. This is what facilitates the flow. This is the way to reach up high.

And this, I believe, is how to find the happily ever after without having to be Cinderella at all.

Motivation

*Even though we sometimes would not get a thing, we were happy with the joy
the day would bring.*

~I WISH, STEVIE WONDER

I have given my children an assignment.

And that is to send me photos of buddhas from their travels in and around
New York City.

Buddhas have become an item of interest for me, and I figure I'll need the
photos for my blog. Hopefully, just knowing they are on their way will help
motivate me.

But sometimes it can be hard to get up and go, to actually start the day. It
might be raining. It might be too hot. There might be hiccups like not enough
sleep, too many responsibilities, or some daunting tasks.

Or there could just be too much humidity, like the other day when I received a
photo of my daughter, a mass of curls atop her head with a text that simply said,
Help!

When I called, laughing, she announced, *It's not funny! This is how I look! I can't go
outside!*

Many of my days include going to yoga, and so I am easily motivated to start
the day.

My son works around the clock and around the week and often runs on
minimal sleep. On some days, his motivation is elusive. On those mornings, he
calls just to help himself wake up.

During such calls, I mostly talk and threaten to sing my good morning song
from the movie *Anchors Away*, with Gene Kelly and Debbie Reynolds, while he

makes some unintelligible sounds. The pseudo-conversation ends when I ask, *Are you vertical?* If the answer is affirmative, the call is over. If not, I start to sing.

Even if motivation is missing, it can be worthwhile to start the day just to see what's in store. It's like that with a yoga practice, too. In fact, my best practices show up on those rare occasions when my motivation is lacking.

Many times, especially when my children were little, we wouldn't even know what the day would bring. Often we'd be doing something unexpected by the day's end, and it would always be a welcome surprise.

Like the time we wound up in New York City for the day, still in pajamas because we left so early on the spur of the moment. Or when we dropped our afternoon plans to lay in sleeping bags under the skylights for an unexpected and gigantic late-day thunderstorm. Or when we did the same, but this time outside on the driveway at three in the morning for a meteor shower.

And on those days, I would exclaim, *We didn't know when we woke up that we'd be doing this!*

Today, I send my children this same message when they look to me for motivation as young adults. Now I tell them, *Just see what the day brings.* And that is often reason enough to get up and go, especially when one's motivation is still under the pillow.

I was in a store the other day, and there was a sign behind the cash register that read, *Have you woken up two days in a row uninspired? Change your life!*

I think that's a tall order, although not a bad contemplation. More manageable might be just to have some faith in the day and see what it brings, whether or not big life changes are in order.

For me, I hope it brings a photo of a buddha from New York City.

Walking Tall

Walk tall in the power day after day. Never, never, never lose sight of the way.

~WALK IN THE POWER, ELTON JOHN AND LITTLE RICHARD

Standing on your hands in class does not make you a better yogi. What makes you a better yogi is standing on your own two feet in the chaos of the street.

These were the words of my daughter's yoga instructor one summer morning when she finally, triumphantly, nailed a handstand.

Surroundings can impact us.

Many emergency rooms are painted in greens and blues, colors that create a sense of calm. Some restaurants have patterned floors to encourage diners to eat quickly so that more people can be seated. And most people accent their homes with photographs, paintings, books and whatever else creates for them a comforting surrounding. I've even heard it said that the colors in a home should match whatever looks good on the owners, so the owners themselves feel more at home!

The walls of many yoga studios are painted in calming colors and accented with murals of buddhas and bamboo, gods and goddesses, lotuses and Oms and more. From my mat, the poses provide various vantage points as the murals come into view, decorating my practice from different directions.

One such mural had even helped me practice my inversions. It was a bamboo mural with its brown shoots standing tall and straight, divided into segments and stacked one atop another. I used this mural to land upside down, visualizing the bamboo as I moved into my handstands, stacking each part of my body, one atop another, mirroring the mural.

To teach handstand, the instructor would often refer to Tadasana, or

Mountain pose. In Tadasana, the feet are together, big toes touching. The body stands tall, the neck is long, the shoulders are down and the arms are by the sides, hands splayed out and palms facing forward. All points on the body are stacked, one atop another, like the bamboo in the mural. Feet and legs line up directly below the hips; torso and shoulders line up directly above.

Handstand is just Tadasana upside down.

My daughter had spent quite some time conquering her fear of inversions and had finally tackled her headstand before progressing to handstands. The challenge was twofold: keeping the fear of inverting at bay, and landing the balance in the pose itself.

One morning, she accompanied me to class and, during the inversion segment, the instructor came over to assist, demonstrating a step that would allow her to stack her body upside down and linger for a moment. He placed his hands on the mat, lifted one leg to the ceiling and tucked the other inward, bent at the knee. Upside down, he lingered, hip points and shoulders stacked, all but one knee in line with the rest of his body.

Just practice like that, he said, encouraging her not to complete the handstand by leaving one leg bent. After several attempts, my daughter lingered, too, hanging like an upside down bamboo shoot. Later, she declared the class more than worth waking up for.

By summer's end, not long after, she had her triumphant day. When she called to tell me about it, I could hear the chaos of her city surroundings as she navigated her errands while calmly relating her handstand achievement.

You're an amazing yogi! I exclaimed. *You stood on your hands!*

Mom, she countered as she echoed her instructor's words, *I'm a good yogi for being on my feet in these crazy streets!*

I laughed in response because I knew that, even so, it was her hands that had served as the good start to this day, and her feet were just what followed.

Inner Strength

Here's what we call our golden rule. Have faith in you and the things you do. You won't go wrong.

~WE ARE FAMILY, SISTER SLEDGE

There is a pose in yoga called Tadasana, otherwise known as Mountain pose.

In Tadasana, we move to the top of our mats and just stand there straight and tall. Nothing fancy. No twists. No binds. No balancing. We even get to close our eyes. It sounds simple enough to just stand there, but actually a lot is going on.

I always feel as if I am building this pose, bit by bit. The instructor usually runs down a checklist of the body. First, we stand as tall as possible, with our feet rooted into the ground and our necks stretched long. Then, we press our shoulders down with our arms along our sides. We face our palms forward and reach through the fingertips.

We draw in our bellies, close our eyes and breathe.

I find this pose fortifying. It makes me feel relaxed but also makes me feel strong. It gives me a sense of myself and makes me feel at peace.

I was lucky enough to have grown up in a supportive family which fostered a strong sense of self. But it has been a long time since then and, in my adult years, I have sometimes needed to resurrect this sense of self. It's always inside, but at times like in Mountain pose, I have to go back to rebuilding it, bit by bit.

Tadasana provides the hidden inner strength in most yoga poses. So we can be in an inversion and find Tadasana while upside down. Or we can be in Plank and find Tadasana while horizontal. We can also be in Extended Side Angle and find Tadasana on a tilt.

No matter the position, there is a bit of Tadasana holding us in place.

Self-doubt is the nemesis of inner strength and, here and there, I have found myself in times of doubt which have made me feel upside down or, at the very least, on a tilt.

It can be a challenge to find my footing again, but I have done so by going through my own checklist of sorts. Sometimes finding my footing can involve retreating a bit for some time on my own.

I remember when I was a new mom at 25 years old. None of my other friends were moms at that young age. After a few years, we moved to the suburbs. When I joined a playgroup, I finally met some other mothers my age.

And it was in their company that I realized I was out of sync with my decision to wait another year before sending my first child to nursery school. My daughter could not even talk yet, and I wanted to wait until she could tell me about her day.

That was actually the first time I encountered some doubts about a direction I had chosen. I left the group early that day and remember going home and pausing alone in my foyer, finding my own reasons for my choice.

I had to tap into myself, and I stuck with my decision.

We usually arrive at Tadasana after working up quite a sweat in the practice, and it can be a welcome reprieve. It is a kind of regrouping, like standing in the foyer before continuing on.

It's strange how it's taken yoga to make me realize that I can take Tadasana anytime I want, that there is always the opportunity to rebuild my sense of self when I believe it has gone missing.

It is always there inside, even when I have my doubts.

Truth 8

Love can be possible
when the heart is opened.

Open Heart

Love is the opening door. Love is what we came here for.

~LOVE SONG, ELTON JOHN

I would like to say I have an open heart.

It sounds nice and like something I should have. Blessed with family and friends, I have people in my life for whom I open my heart.

Yet the heart can go through some rough terrain over a period of time, and it can cause the guard gates to go up, requiring encouragement and often a leap of faith to get back in gear.

Wheel is one of my least favorite poses in yoga. It is a backbend, something I had not done since I was a little girl.

More than 20 years ago, I sprained my lower back and have since been on guard against it getting hurt again. After an emergency trip to the hospital and several weeks laid up, I was finally rescued by an osteopath who, mercifully, tweaked my back with some gentle pressure, allowing me to reach my toes for the first time in weeks.

Needless to say, when I first started yoga and the instructor announced it was time for Wheel, I balked. Laying there on the mat, I told him I did not really twist. Nor did I bend like that. I was on guard for fear of my back.

He stood above my head, looked down at me and told me to brace myself on his ankles. He leaned down and scooped me up under my upper back and, voila! I was in a backbend, albeit with some support. This went on for a few classes until I realized I did not have to fear my back, and soon I could lift up into a backbend on my own.

Next, I was encouraged to try a variation: to go into a backbend and lift one leg, hold it for a beat or two, put it down, and do the same with the other. I had seen this done by others in the room but, again, my guard was up. I could not even get the toes of one foot off the ground.

Once more, the instructor encouraged me. He stood alongside me and placed his knee under my back. With his support, I was able to lift my leg and hold it for that beat. Soon after, I could do this on my own.

In yoga, it is believed that there are seven main chakras, or energy centers, located along the spinal column. Coincidentally, chakra is the Sanskrit word for Wheel. If balanced, these energy centers spin in wheel-like circles, and all is well emotionally, physically, intellectually and spiritually.

However, if we navigate some rough terrain, some of these chakras can become blocked, and it is the yoga poses that help open them and get the energy flowing properly once more.

The fourth chakra is the Heart Chakra, located at the center of the chest. It is associated with love and trust, and the first step in its healing is to find faith and love for oneself. The yoga pose associated with releasing any blockage in this chakra just happens to be Wheel.

There is yet another way to get into Wheel, and it starts on the knees in a pose called Camel. Hands are placed in prayer at heart center before the body tilts back and goes overboard, the hands slowly extending up and over the head and finally finding the floor behind the feet. The knees come up off the ground and the body winds up in Wheel.

The motion is fluid, but there is a moment of limbo before the knees are up, before the hands are on the ground, before the body is safely positioned.

Once again, the instructor stood nearby, verbally guiding me through the motion. In the split second that I realized I was in limbo, and in the millisecond that I was deciding to bail, he encouraged me, saying, *Keep going, keep going, keep going!* That was all I needed to make that leap of faith to land my hands.

I was safe. I was in Wheel.

Soon after, I confessed to the instructor that Wheel was my least favorite pose. *Heart opener,* was all he said.

I got the message. Those two words summed up the necessary work to lower the guard gates and get my heart in gear.

Fear

How to be brave? How to love when I'm afraid to fall?

~A THOUSAND YEARS, CHRISTINA PERRI

I'm hoping the third time's a charm.

I hit my head at yoga. Then I did it again and shortly thereafter did it once more. These three hits happened, accidentally on purpose, as part of my efforts to drop into a backbend from standing.

It's scary, but I'm not ready to stop. I console myself with the thought that hitting one's head is supposed to happen in threes, so hopefully, I've also hit my quota.

I'm not sure why I feel so compelled to get into a backbend in this way when I can get there in other ways. I can't really identify my incentive, but I feel like it's a barrier that I have to break.

I also must confess that this might partly be a quest by the high achiever that happens to reside inside this sometimes fearful girl.

What I do know is that it's not really so yogic to push as if I'm on some kind of impatient mission. And I know I'm not supposed to fight to get a pose, but that hasn't stopped me from setting a deadline to win this battle.

My best guess is that backbends are supposed to be about opening the heart, and the dipping back is supposed to be about facing fears. So maybe on some level I am trying to do both.

It's a surrendering. And I think that's my barrier. It's risky to surrender.

I do take the instructor's words to heart when he says to *crack open your chest* when we bend back in any fashion. This imagery really works for me, helping me to lean farther and farther back, to lift my heart up and back, to lift my arms and to stretch out of my lower back and get a good look at the wall behind me.

My heart has been closed for business for a long time. Maybe that's my barrier, too.

Several times a week at the end of class, the instructor dips me back three or four times. That's when I hit my head for the first time, even though I landed my hands.

We've been doing this for a few months, and now he says he is spotting me less and less. I have a much better feel now for how I need to ground myself more in my feet, tighten more in my core, and straighten more in my arms in order to make a safe and strong landing.

The other day, I arrived home after a good practice, thinking the time has got to come when I risk dipping back on my own.

And I decided that time could be now. I could surrender now.

So I laid out my mat, put a chair cushion in the middle as a safety net and set myself up to dip back, on my own, all by myself. Ever so slowly, I reached up and bent back, back, back, until I passed the point of no return and landed my hands with a bounce.

A big day! I could even do it again and again!

I took that confidence to class the next day, only to have it buoy me for one, but not for another, when I landed my hands but then bounced on my head. Hit number two. The instructor made me do it again for the very reason I hit my head.

Another day, another class, another try. And that's when I reached my quota, hitting my head for the third time.

And now I feel like I've hit some sort of wall, even though it's really just the mat. I'm scared to try again. This has turned into a bit of an emotional endeavor without too much rational thought, the existence of which may be moot, anyway, should I keep hitting my head!

But what I do know is that I need to keep trying. I want to get to the other side of that barrier and see what's there.

Nose Dive

Sweet dreams 'til sunbeams find you. Sweet dreams leave worries behind you.

~DREAM A LITTLE DREAM OF ME, THE MAMAS AND THE PAPAS

From the time I was little, I was taught to stand up straight and sit up straight.

I remember in my little-girl ballet classes, when we folded forward we had to hold the fold so straight that even the teacher's lipstick case would not roll off our backs.

Summers would find me at camp, seated with my bunkmates on benches instead of chairs at each meal. I remember partway through one summer the counselor looking at all of us hunched there, and exclaiming, *You all started out sitting up so straight and now look at you!* We rose to better attention and for the rest of the summer made a conscious effort to sit up straight.

And, yes, a la Marcia and Jan Brady, I even spent several months with my sister going to what we called *Charm School,* where we walked around balancing books on our heads.

Today there are studies about the positive effects of a positive posture. Posture can be what it takes to fake it 'til we make it on any given day, because how we carry ourselves is how we care for ourselves. After all, what's being lifted when we hold ourselves up are our hearts, so there's really no better reason to not be slouching around.

So now with ballet and camp and charm school in the past, I turn to yoga to straighten up.

At yoga, there is lots of talk about the heart and, before we even start, we are called to the top of our mats and told to stand up straight. We pull in our bellies and push down our shoulders. We reach up, lift up, and look up.

And it's no matter how hunched I might have been before, or for how long, because the practice gives me the chance to stand up straight again and again, and that only feels good.

It has taken me a long time to fall in love with any of the heart-opening poses where we lift or puff out our chests. But now I even like leaning back, so my heart flows up and over and almost overboard.

One class I take on a regular basis emphasizes this intuitive link between movement and the heart. For me, this class seems to help close the gap between the young girl who always knew to sit up straight and the older one who, at times, can forget to walk tall.

The class is slow-going and hard-working. We reach and stretch and pull ourselves into postures, and we are reminded to have our hearts like Sphinx, the pose where, even low to the ground, the shoulders are back and the chest is lifted.

Around and around we go, following our hearts to the front of the mat and then to the back, stopping each time to open and lift to one side or the other.

We even do something called Toppling Tree, moving through a series of balances on one foot only to wind up with the other high in the air behind us, our bodies in a nose dive with our chests lifted and leading the way to the mat.

And, surprisingly, it's there in the nose dive where all my caution disappears. I come to stillness while soaring toward the mat as my arms and shoulders pull back with my chest pressed forward in this one big tilt that's led by the heart.

By the time we get to the part where we put our hands on our hips and turn out our toes to lean back, I find I can lift my heart high enough and lean back far enough to get a full-on look at the wall behind me. And I wonder if I'm overboard enough to put my hands down for Wheel, or if my heart is just telling me so.

And after, when it's time for the ending backbends, mine come easily and without any usual stiffness.

If movement and the heart are linked, then I guess I can liken caring for my heart to walking with a cupful of coffee and no cover. I'd have to tread lightly so as not to spill. And that's a pretty daunting analogy because I've always been a big spiller!

Regardless, in this class, it's as if I'm filled to the brim but able to move without a lid. I think that's how I wound up so happy in the nose dive.

At the end of class, we are asked to sit up straight with our hands at our hearts. And without further ado or the usual closing, the instructor imparts a simple message.

He says only: *You all will have sweet dreams tonight.*

And this simple declaration actually comes true. That night, I close my eyes for a dream where I'm practicing the same circular motions in the same roundabout flow, my heart lifted by the movements for another chance to stand up straight, again and again, even in my sleep.

Seeing Stars

Have you ever thrown a fistful of glitter in the air? Have you ever looked fear in the face and said I just don't care?

~GLITTER IN THE AIR, PINK

I've been seeing stars at yoga.

As soon as you see the floor, put your hands down!

The instructor is standing in front of me, holding my hips. My hands are in prayer at my heart. The plan is for me to bend backward and look for the floor, tilting over and saving myself last minute with my hands.

I think most people can probably identify a time when they've had to save themselves at the last minute. Such challenges can just be part of life, the part where you learn, where your head spins and you see stars.

So now I've been living yoga for the better part of a few years, and I've definitely learned a lot, mostly because I started out knowing nothing. Basic poses, advanced poses, arm balances and inversions. There are lots of challenges, and no matter how accomplished I might become, there is forever room to learn more. There is something called full expression, which is as far as a pose can go, but even once that's accomplished, it can always be taken a little deeper.

It seems the poses that challenge me the most are those I want most to achieve, and I want to face them head on. I am not sure how yogic that is, to speak of achieving. We are taught to be okay with the present moment, that we are enough for now, and that everything is already okay.

But what about challenging myself and striving to overcome obstacles? And what if those obstacles happen to be a handstand in the middle of the room, and dropping into a backbend from standing? I can't do either, but I want to, and soon! To me, it's not enough to try or wonder if it will happen.

The floor comes at me fast, and I pop open my hands to land on the mat. I think I've done okay, but I can't find my way back up. The instructor pulls me up and forward, doing all the heavy lifting. Once upright, I get a head rush, and it's an effort to listen to his advice on how to better come up. I even see a few stars while letting the rush pass by.

Walk your hands closer to your feet and power up your legs, he says. *Put all the weight in your quads and press into your feet to rise up.*

I am at what I hope is midlife, and this is what I've chosen as my next big challenge! Those around me say I have another challenge. I am single. I have raised two children. I write. I paint. I have a job. And I am learning yoga. Those around me want me to have more. They want me to have someone in my life.

On the second try, the instructor puts a strap around my lower back, and we face each other while he holds either end.

Okay, now. Go back.

I'm going back.

Okay, just go back.

Just go back? Just go right back? Okay, I'm going back.

We have this ricochet conversation, and then I tilt back. The floor comes up fast again, and I pop open my hands to land them once more on the mat. This time feels easier. Maybe it's my imagination, but I don't think I leaned too much into the strap. I am still unable to lift myself back up, and the instructor hoists me to vertical again. A second head rush. More stars.

For me, the thought of having someone in my life is daunting. I've been going it alone for quite some time, but I guess I've been more curious these days, and maybe that's why I'm getting so much encouragement. But venturing *out there* is like tilting back with no one holding my hips. I could crash and burn.

The instructor smiles a lot. He is encouraging. He sets it up so it feels safe to go back. I tell him I plan to nail this pose by my next birthday, five months away. It's probably not so yogic to set a deadline, but I want this sooner than later.

For the rest of it, I don't think I need a deadline in order to face it head on. I think, instead, I'll just set it in my sights until it feels safe enough to try.

Spider and Fly

Unchain my heart. Let me go my way.

~UNCHAIN MY HEART, RAY CHARLES

Come into my parlor, said the spider to the fly.

This phrase references a poem by Mary Howitt published in 1829 about a naïve fly ensnared by a less than honest spider.

A warning to the naïve, this phrase has twice been directed at me.

I have met some spiders in my time; but I really never thought myself to be the fly. Why, then, have I bumped up against these words more than once?

The first time, I had walked down the wedding aisle and had just arrived under the *Chuppah*, the Jewish wedding canopy. Inside waiting to greet us stood the rabbi.

He looked at me with a twinkle in his eye and said softly, *Come into my parlor, said the spider to the fly.*

Ten years later, I heard this phrase again. I had walked down the hall and had just arrived at my meeting. Inside waiting to greet me stood my divorce attorney.

He looked at me with a twinkle in his eye and said softly, *Come into my parlor, said the spider to the fly.*

Coincidence? I think not!

Do any of us ever really consider ourselves naïve? Maybe in hindsight but for me, in the moment, I usually think I know what's going on. It's only afterward that I'm aware I might not have been so savvy.

I wonder where this greeting was when I signed up for yoga. I had thought yoga was just exercise. I was surprised to find it was so much more, and now I think I am ensnared for life. I had no idea that the practice would push at me, and

I am far from savvy about the direction in which I am headed.

As a young adult, I had a certain naiveté of which I was unaware, an oxymoron in itself. I readily trusted, honestly believed and openly embraced. But some spiders since have taught me about the need for balance between trust and skepticism, between faith and cynicism. You've got to have a little of each.

The other day at the end of my yoga practice, the instructor gave a reading. We lay in our final resting pose of Savasana, the practice over. The readings really work for me at this point because, for the moment, the practice erases all skepticism and cynicism. I lay there on my mat with only trust and faith. And I feel good.

The reading spoke to the importance of opening our hearts to love, even if we have been hurt. Even if it means being vulnerable. Even if opening our hearts and being vulnerable is what got us hurt in the first place.

This is all food for thought and sort of difficult to put into practice. It seems I equate vulnerability with naiveté, and for me there seems to be a challenge in how to avoid the fate of the fly when opening the heart.

For some reason, I think yoga is teaching me how to do this. And even though I have been writing on the subject for a while, it's difficult to find the words to explain.

I just know to keep going back to the mat.

It's not just that I *want* to practice; it's that I *have* to practice. There is something about it that pulls me closer to myself, and that, I think, is what may ultimately make it safe to be anywhere near vulnerable again.

At one point, I had a private lesson where the instructor was running me through the poses. I was in Trikonasana, or Triangle pose, tilted to the side with one arm to the floor and the other to the sky. I pushed my lower ribs forward and pulled my top ribs back, tilting toward the ceiling.

You have a very open heart, said the instructor.

This was news to me, but I was on my mat with not a spiderweb in sight.

Love

Sometimes we misplace things, and sometimes we search for a place to put them.

With love, I have done both.

I have always had a lot of love to give. I have nourished my children with it. I can see the results in their kindness and generosity and in the beautiful young adults they have become. It has been easy to love my family, my relatives, my friends, and my colleagues.

I am able to give a certain type of love to those I do not even know, and the capacity to do so comes through the compassion and empathy I have for others.

You are my guardian angel, says one such stranger. I found her stranded in her car in a rainstorm. She is 90. Now she wants to make me lunch.

The love I put out into the world makes its way back to me tenfold, and I feel cared for by so many people in my life. For this, I am grateful.

But there is another kind of love that is not so easy to give. It's the kind that makes me vulnerable. It's fragile, and it's sort of in pieces.

It is hard to figure out how to mend it and share it again. What about the pieces? I would not even know where to begin. They were swept aside so long ago into a nice neat pile, untouched in the corner of my consciousness.

The only thing I can think of is to leave them and go from there, and I think my yoga practice is helping me do that. For some reason, moving on the mat is like turning on the lights. The more I move, the brighter it gets.

My practice has led me to some healers, one in particular who wants me to turn on even more light.

I have been advised to imagine a cord of energy from myself to the past, cutting it, and then visualizing a healing green light over the imagined wound. Next, I am supposed to see in my mind's eye a maternal pink light wrapping itself around me, and then, on top of that, a protective white light.

I have my doubts about this, but I have to admit that I have imagined these lights twice so far. The green light makes me feel a bit wistful, the pink light makes me feel calm, and the white light makes me feel strong.

Maybe the first step in figuring all this out is to simply open up to the idea of having to heal in the first place. Before starting my yoga practice, I honestly did not know I had any healing to do. I had thought it was my idea not to let anyone too close. I didn't realize I had any work to do first.

It takes a lot of courage to turn on these lights, green, pink, white or whatever other color, and even more to face whatever it is they may spotlight. Even so, I think they might help illuminate what's been missing.

And, who knows, maybe what's been missing is me. Maybe, just maybe, this love is a gift I can give myself.

Truth 9

Trust can be fostered
when the present moment is validated.

Stuck

The past is gone. It went by like dusk to dawn. Isn't that the way?

~DREAM ON, AEROSMITH

If you think back to where you started, you can always find the joy in where you are.

This is how the instructor opened the morning's yoga class. This instructor is such a young man, and I can't figure out how he has such insights at half my age.

This is what my grandmother always told me, he said.

Aha!

Interestingly enough, that morning I had awakened thinking about how far I had *not* come. All I could think of was how stuck I was, and the day hadn't even started. How did I wake up stuck?

On my more enlightened days, I know I have journeyed many miles and have much to show for it. But that morning the light wasn't really on, and I almost got stuck in the bed. I made some coffee, which flipped the switch, and so I put on my yoga clothes and headed out.

The route I take to yoga always makes me think about my starting point, or, really, a few starting points. I grew up where I now live, and to get to yoga I have to drive many miles alongside the water, next to the canal that's next to the river. The journey is a straight shot down memory lane.

It's a spring-like day, even though it is not yet mid-March, and the river is unusually calm and green. I open my sunroof and turn on the radio. The music, the sun and the river brighten this day's light all the more.

As a little girl, I would climb the rocks at the river on family outings, just a little ways up from where my drive begins. I remember the rocks being so huge and feeling so big when I reached the top. We'd search for flat stones and skip them forever, counting the pops off the water. I also remember finding long sticks with my brother and sister and being so proud when mine was the tallest, as if I myself had grown as tall as the stick.

I was little, and the little things I was doing made me feel overall adventurous and pretty big.

Farther along, I pass my old neighborhood where my children were born. I see our favorite restaurant, and there's the library. The theater is now a pharmacy, and there's the post office.

I remember holding hands with my daughter and seeing our reflection in that post office window. I was a young mom, and the picture of us in the window made me feel overall adventurous and pretty big, all over again.

I've taken my children to the water many times. We'd celebrate the last day of school during their elementary years with a trip to the water to feed the geese. Lots of times we'd rent canoes and paddle around, or ride the barge. Once the canal froze over, and we hopped in the car for a chance to walk on the water among the skaters.

I arrive downtown and pass what used to be the printer's shop where I'd often go in an old life, and I park by the water on a little side street that my now-adult son earlier scouted out for me. I get out of the car, look over the water and walk to the studio.

The drive alone is good for me and so is the brief walk. It's no surprise that I feel a connection here; the studio sits right on the water alongside the canal. I'm early, and the young girl who manages the front desk is standing outside in her bare feet with her iPad.

You're checked in, Anne, she says. *I saw you at the top of the street.*

I thank her and tell her I'm going to sit by the canal for a bit.

I come to yoga to get unstuck. That's what the practice is all about, clearing the chakras, or energy centers, with the asanas, or poses. But, really, I think the instructor's words come true just on the ride here. The view outside the car window is like a movie reel, showcasing my many miles.

And I arrive right where I am, with the joy of no longer wondering about my finish line, where it should be or why I may not have crossed it just yet.

Sweet Spot

An' living ain't so bad without a rudder.

~PAPER CUP, FIFTH DIMENSION

Handstands make me happy. It sounds odd, but it's true!

I remember well the practice where we incorporated handstands at the start of our vinyasas, the transition sequence of which we do many, giving us lots of opportunities to invert.

For me, it was great fun, and I couldn't believe how elated I'd get over it. Really, I never thought that I'd be happiest upside down, but this is so, and the feeling lasts long past the time I'm upright again.

Incorporating handstands changed up the same-old, and with them the vinyasas offered up opportunities and challenges as they hadn't before.

In general, I'm getting better and better at changes. Just the other morning, someone I know well was telling me how much he likes structure in his life. I was surprised to hear this as to me he always seems so spontaneous, always making me feel like the one who needs a plan.

I was even more surprised to hear myself tell him that these days I find freedom in just being, in not always knowing my next step.

I used to be a big planner; now, not so much. I find this helps me move more easily through my life's flow. Now I have come to appreciate the benefits of not always knowing, or having to know, what comes next.

When I learned the handstand vinyasas, I'd practice them up against the wall. This helped in case I lost my balance. After one or two regular vinyasas, I'd start to incorporate the handstand.

Going for the handstand was always touch and go. My objectives were to invert without using the wall, even though it was right there, and to find the sweet spot and just hang. Sometimes it worked and sometimes it didn't. And it was kind of fun not knowing what would happen.

Once upon a time, I was all about lining things up. My work life, my home life, my personal life. And for a long time, for the most part, life did line up according to what I considered my plan. But at some point I came to realize there were just too many things beyond my control and that it was best to let go a little, if not a lot.

In this way, I sort of set myself free, and it's taught me to be okay with not knowing every outcome in the face of change.

In learning the handstand vinyasas, the best feeling would come when not much effort was applied, when I would just kick up and let one foot meet the other in midair. I never knew if I would find the balance until I did, and when I did it was always a sweet surprise.

The practice allowed for us to hold the handstand if we found the balance and to come down in our own time, even if the class had already moved ahead. I found that, on those occasions when I'd nail it, I could linger in that sweet spot for some length of time, especially if I wasn't too distracted.

The instructor would encourage us to remain in our handstands by saying, *Keep on going!* Yet what I really heard in those words were instructions to land in the moment whenever we could and stay there for as long as we could.

Learning the handstand vinyasas taught me to be grateful for when I do find the sweet spot, and it helped me recognize that hanging there is often easiest to do when free of any what-ifs and what-nots.

The other day, I bought my daughter a card. The words that filled the front read: *Yesterday is history. Tomorrow is mystery. Today is a gift.*

I think today is the sweet spot.

Gratitude

Take your time. Don't live too fast. Troubles will come, and they will pass.

~SIMPLE MAN, LYNYRD SKYNYRD

I was trying to make a late evening yoga class, and it was a bit bumpy getting there.

I am a suburbanite who has found some classes downtown, and in the evening when there's no traffic, I can zip down there fairly quickly. The studio is hot, the people are warm, and the energy is high. I love stepping in.

But the other night the road was literally blocked, and I had to take a detour. *Why am I doing this?* I asked myself.

Instead of coming up with an answer, a calmness settled in, and I turned on the radio and took the alternate route. I arrived at the cash-only parking lot with 15 minutes to spare before realizing I had left my cash at home.

Why am I doing this? I asked myself again.

But the attendant was kind, saw my yoga mat on my back and told me about the nearby ATM, asking first if getting cash would make me late for class.

Again, a calmness settled in, and I said, *No worries, I have time.*

I'm not sure from where the evening's calmness came, but I had apparently left the house with it. Ordinarily, I would have been frustrated by the hiccups encountered thus far.

I finally stepped into the studio, put up my hair and laid out my mat in the front of the room. I am sort of claustrophobic, and it helps not to have the crowd in front of me.

Shortly before the class started, I turned around. The room was packed, mostly with college students from the nearby university.

Why am I doing this? I asked myself again.

I said to the man next to me, *This room is so young!* A moment later, he leaned over and whispered back, *You are still not as old as me!* And with those encouraging words, the practice began.

The instructor was generous and engaging and motivating, and the practice was vigorous. At the end, that same calmness washed over me.

And it was then that I finally understood about the practice creating space. For me, and on that night in particular, the physical workout of yoga seems to create an opening inside, and I am left in Savasana, or final resting pose, with a feeling of being smoothed out, almost like a chalkboard with the scribbles now erased.

The instructor gave a reading while we lay there at the end, and I cannot for the life of me remember the details. I only remember that I liked hearing the words, and that they were words of kindness and support.

I just lay there at the end on my mat with an immense and unexpected gratitude. And that is what filled the space created by the practice.

Afterward, the man next to me leaned over again and said, *See? You are younger now!*

I am thinking he must have felt it, too! And it occurred to me that gratitude might well be like feeling younger, like opening to a time when optimism and hopefulness ruled the day.

The studio was just about empty, and so I moved my mat to the wall to practice a handstand before leaving. I pressed my hands to the mat, lifted one leg and then the other and locked in my core for the strongest handstand I'd had in some time.

And there, upside down, the evening's calmness that had accompanied me earlier returned once more, and I experienced that same immense and unexpected gratitude.

Shortly thereafter, I packed up my things, making sure to include that gratitude. I wanted to take it with me so that I could have it for next time, too.

Neil Young

Tell me why, tell me why ...

~TELL ME WHY, NEIL YOUNG

Neil Young spoke to me the other day.

Not directly and not exactly, but I did hear him! It happened on an unusual day which allowed for midday yoga, a rarity and a treat.

Earlier that day, I caught an interview on television with the singer and songwriter, Neil Young. I had forgotten all about him and how much I loved his voice! I made a mental note to download some of his songs.

The interviewer asked Neil Young about his life. Were his songs autobiographical? The singer hemmed and hawed, explaining that his songs came from inside, so inherent in each was indeed some truth. And, he admitted, not all his songs were so rosy.

The interviewer pressed further but received a cryptic answer.

It's not all great, but I'm sure glad to be here while it's happening.

I made a written note of this concisely stated truth and went to yoga.

Over the few months prior, there had been some losses. People I thought would still be around no longer were. Losses like these had made me think about the grand scheme of things and also about my own health. And the thought of both had made me recommit to my yoga practice.

I walked into midday yoga and set up my mat. The background music caught me by surprise. I had not heard the studio play this artist in all the time I had been practicing.

We have a little Neil Young playing, the instructor said as he walked over to switch up the songs and start the practice.

Turns out, Neil had a lot to say that day. Coincidence? Kabbalah, the study of Jewish mysticism, would say there is no such thing.

I have my own philosophy about such synchronicity. I take it as a sign that I'm doing what I'm supposed to be doing at the time I'm supposed to be doing it.

So I figured I was supposed to be standing there in that studio on my mat, caring for my body and for my spirit. Because in the vein of that grand scheme of things, what is the good in having strong muscles without a strong spirit?

Any losses can create questions that seem too big for answers. The other day, out of nowhere, someone actually asked me why I thought I was here. More specifically, I was asked what I thought was my intended soul correction, another concept of Kabbalah.

Really, I had no answer. And I think it can take at least a lifetime to try to figure that one out. The best I can do is just pay attention, be grateful and not take anything for granted.

I wanted to explain to my fellow yogis about Neil Young, but how would I even begin to do that? Instead, I just completed my practice, finished my day, and that night downloaded the singer's songs, *Harvest Moon* and *After the Gold Rush*.

Later that week, I was not surprised to find that Neil Young had moved from the background music to a spot on that day's yoga practice playlist.

I just looked up from my mat and exclaimed, *Neil Young!*

Certainty

Trust your intuition. It's just like going fishing. You cast your line and hope you get a bite.

~FATHER AND DAUGTHER, PAUL SIMON

I have always had a bit of a sixth sense, but that doesn't mean I can see the future or always pave what I think might be a good path.

This heightened intuition is a knowing that is difficult to describe. The best I can do is to say that if a truth could be touched, it would feel like this. This might sound vague, yet the feeling is anything but.

When I am practicing yoga, I can experience a sensation similar to this sixth sense. In a pose or after a practice, a calmness comes at me, and I feel centered and light and surprised. It's like the feeling I get when an old favorite song comes on the radio. *Oh, I know this!*

I was at yoga the other night, and the instructor was all excited about the new funky music playing. I approved, as I had just added Stevie Wonder to my personal playlist, and Stevie and his friends had been serenading me at home.

I was in a handstand, killing time after practice while awaiting some instruction on backbends. I moved my mat to the wall and pressed into my hands, lifting first one leg and then the other. Usually it takes a few tries, but this time right away my legs found their hang, and I was easily upside down.

Instead of feeling my weight in my hands, though, I felt no weight at all. That calmness came at me, and I felt centered and light and surprised. I felt such certainty in that moment, upside down.

How is it that such clarity and certainty are never the result of a conscious effort? It's not like I sit down and decide to come up with an answer to something that I don't even know is on my mind. It just happens out of the blue, in the same sudden way as easily landing that handstand.

The only conclusion I've been able to come to is that when I am clear of concerns, an openness is created. I get a filled-up feeling, and that's when the answers come. It's when I know what I know. It's the time to write. It's the time to paint. It's the time to listen.

The instructor came over to help me drop into a backbend from standing. We were giving it three tries after every practice. Stevie Wonder blasted through the sound system, and I got that feeling. I placed my hands at my heart, told the instructor that Stevie had followed me here from home and dropped back with more certainty than ever before.

Of course it goes without saying that these times of certainty can be counterbalanced by bouts of uncertainty, when I wonder if I am headed in the best direction or if tilting back is even a good idea at all. It's the wondering that gets in the way, the overthinking that closes the open space where the answers come in.

Before yoga I had never exercised, and I can't believe I missed out on all those years of using this method as a means to make sense of myself. A lot of confusion gets worked out on my mat. The practice clears away the chaos by moving me out of my head and into my body, making room for any answers that might make themselves known.

I arrive home to shower, not at all surprised to turn on my music and find Stevie still with me, finishing the exact same song that took me back at yoga.

The shower has also been the source of several epiphanies. I guess hot hard water pressing down on me does the same thing as my yoga practice. Standing there, I've definitely had a calmness come at me. A realization occurs, I feel centered, light and surprised, and I am certain of a new truth.

Kabbalah, the study of Jewish mysticism, teaches about something called the Certainty Principle. It exists where we can't see, and it's supposed to help in facing difficult situations. According to Yehuda Berg, author of *The Power of Kabbalah*, the principle goes like this: *When challenges appear overwhelming, inject Certainty. The Light is always there.*

There is a lot of study behind the Kabbalistic principles, but a down and dirty broad stroke would be to say there is a lot we don't know, and don't need to know, in order to believe that what's happening is as it should be.

Something is always certain, although I'm not always sure what.

It doesn't escape me that being certain takes some kind of faith. And I do have to admit that I often reach those rare times of utmost certainty only after traveling through some confusion.

Keeping up my yoga practice helps me keep the faith.

And that helps me be open for the centeredness, lightness and surprise for those times like when I reach to reference Berg's book, and somehow open right to the page on Certainty.

False Starts

There are some things I may not know. There are some places, dear Lord, I may not go.

~GOD IS REAL/HARE RAM, KRISHNA DAS

Sometimes we only think we know where we should be.

The other night, for whatever reason, I was not supposed to be at yoga. I don't know why, and I never will, but I was not supposed to be there.

That's not to say I didn't try. Believe me, I did!

In yoga, we're told to trust the process. I've heard this saying many times, but it's only recently that I've begun to understand its meaning. I think it means that we are exactly where we are supposed to be at the time we are there, even if we think we should be elsewhere.

The other night, I got the chance to trust the process.

For whatever reason, my best efforts to get to yoga landed me right back where I started. I don't know why, and I never will, but in the end I think I just have to trust that I was not supposed to be there.

I came home from work and did whatever it is I do when I come home. Per my usual, at seven o'clock that evening, I changed into my yoga clothes and left the house.

I'm an early bird by nature. I have a hard time being late, and to be on time and not early actually takes an effort on my part. Usually, I have an easy drive to yoga, a miraculously easy time finding parking, and I always wind up on my mat at the start of class.

On this beautiful winter night, the sky was clear, the stars were out, and the moon followed me on my drive downtown. It hung low in the sky with a yellowish tinge and served as a backdrop to a pretty strange night of yoga that never was.

I landed a great parking spot, but the meter was broken. Two other yogis were trying to pay as well. No luck for any of us. I hopped back in the car, made an illegal, non-yogic U-turn and parked in another spot across the street behind yet another yogi. This time the meter worked.

Class was starting in 10 minutes, and the line was out the door. At this studio, signing up online does not guarantee a spot, and I chatted with the yogi who had parked in front of me while we slowly inched forward. This part always takes patience. It's where the practice really begins!

We were close enough to the entrance to hear the instructor start the class. And then to my surprise, we were turned away! The room was full. There were no more spots.

On the walk back to our cars, my parking buddy confided that she had a backup plan. I begged her to tell me. I was all set to practice with no place to go.

I don't know if you are as crazy as I am, she replied.

I assured her I was absolutely without a doubt crazy, and she told me about a class starting in 20 minutes across town. So off we went on a second try.

The moon was framed in my car's front window and kept me company as I drove farther downtown to a parking spot right in front of this next studio.

My name was put on a waitlist below that of my new yoga pal's. After intense discussions between the instructor and the front desk, it was determined that there was only one spot left.

It's gotta be hers, I said. After all, this was her back-up plan.

No, it's gotta be hers, she said. *I don't want bad karma! I told her to come!*

Two yogis being too nice.

The front desk assured us that her name was legitimately before mine on the waitlist, and so in she went, and home I went. It had been two hours since I had left for yoga. Driving home, I was reminded of another time I was all dressed up for yoga with no place to go.

It was the previous fall, and I was leaving for an early morning class when I locked myself out of the house without realizing I had access to an extra set of keys in my garage. Fortunately, I had my phone and my coffee and called for someone with a spare. I sat down on my front stoop in the dark with the morning moon for company and missed my class, thinking I was stuck.

Later that same night, I told my friend the story, that I had sat outside that morning with access to my keys the whole time without knowing and without going.

This friend has a beautiful Jamaican accent and calls me *Han*. It was early evening, and the moon had yet to show its face.

Han, he said, *you were not supposed to be at yoga this morning.*

He is not a yogi, but somehow he knew to trust the process. He simply shook his head and smiled knowingly.

There is a reason why, he said, *but we don't get to know it.*

Truth 10

The body can be strengthened
when its capabilities are honored.

Muscles

Shining star come into view. Shine its watchful light on you. Give you strength to carry on. Make your body big and strong.

~SHINING STAR, EARTH, WIND & FIRE

I'm thinking I need some more muscles.

I remember when I started yoga, I stood in a studio with a group of women who had probably been working out for most of their days. It was *Day One* for me. Needless to say, it was pretty intimidating to keep coming back, but I did, and it was a good thing. The practice has redefined me, literally.

Now I've got some muscles, and they've appeared in much the same way as with most things in yoga - they kind of crept up on me. It seems that, just suddenly, there they were! One day, the mirror reflected muscles in my arms, my stomach, my legs, my back.

But the more I try to advance, the more I feel my limits. In one class, in particular, I spend lots of time thinking if only I were stronger, I would get *this*.

This being the arm balances, the handstands, the staying on one side with the weight in one leg while doing all sorts of things before moving to the other side and repeating the same.

I mentioned to the instructor the possibility of lifting some weights.

I'm thinking I'm not strong enough, I said.

You can if you want, she replied, telling me that she did, too. *But you are strong!*

Then I admitted to feeling scrawny, and she suggested I email her to *get rid of the crazies*.

But it's the crazies that make me keep coming back. They're what make me want to invert, to lift myself up on my hands with my legs here and there.

And now I am learning that, as with most things in life, such strength has to come from the core. The instructor talks about zipping it up and putting the belly button to the spine. She calls to us about our upward flying locks when we lift and balance and hang.

Still, in this class I feel my edge, the place where I know I need to add something to what I'm doing so that I can do more.

The other day we were in Navasana, or Boat pose. Sitting on our tail bones, our bodies are in a V shape with our legs and backs straight and our feet in line with our noses. Our hands reach up, and we hold for a count of five.

Then we cross, lock and lift, placing our hands down on either side, crossing our legs and lifting ourselves off the mat, swinging our feet underneath us. Ultimately, we are supposed to land in a handstand, swinging ourselves under and through and unfolding into the inversion.

We're heading to handstand here, the instructor says. *It doesn't matter if you're there yet. Some of us will take another day or another month or another 10 years.*

Huh? No one really calls out in this class, but on hearing this I stood up.

What? I blurted out. *Do you know how old I'll be in 10 years?!?*

It doesn't matter how old you are, the instructor replied. *It matters how strong you are.*

At home, I have these little purple weights. They are eight pounds each. And I have some metal ones that are five pounds each. And some little red three-pounders. Surely something can be done with them.

This yoga is called The Rocket. It's from a branch of yoga called Ashtanga, a style where the student is given a sequence of poses, the progression through which has to be done in order. The student can't move on to the next pose until the previous one is accomplished.

Rocket yoga came about in the 1980s, and it teaches some of these poses without having to satisfy any prerequisites. Bob Weir of the Grateful Dead dubbed it The Rocket because, in his words, *You get there faster.*

In my Rocket class, it often feels like *Day One* all over again. I am in there with those who have been there for a while. And just as when I first started yoga, it can be quite intimidating but, like before, I keep coming back.

And the progress is slow.

So my plan is to lift those purple weights, even though I think the key to my progression lies more in the strength of my core. I am being instructed, as with anything else, to look inside to my very center.

Still, I kind of want to rocket through that part, too. I keep waiting to hear some kind of hint about how to better lift up. Surely I must be missing some kind of clue.

But the only way to fly is to lock and lift. And there's no shortcut around that. The strength in my core has to build in its own time.

So I keep practicing my lock and practicing my patience. And hopefully, if I'm locked and lucky, I'll be able to go back and through and lift myself upside down before 10 years are up.

Injury

Take these broken wings and learn to fly. All your life, you were only waiting for this moment to arise.

~BLACKBIRD, PAUL MCCARTNEY

I needed a backup plan for yoga.

I'd hurt my hand, and the doctor had ordered no yoga for one month.

I'd been practicing for a few years, and this was the first time I would go without yoga for more than a few consecutive days.

The anxiety was starting to build. I had been on a full-speed-ahead yoga schedule, combining two types of practices at three different locations for a total of six times a week.

Coming to a hard stop seemed unimaginable. With this news, I was concerned I would lose my strength and the muscles I'd been building. I would miss all the work I'd been doing on my handstands, not to mention the other parts of my practice.

So in light of these worries, I decided on a new plan, something different and out of the ordinary, something that would set this time apart and move it along as speedily as possible.

This plan was to go *outside*, to walk and even run, and then to treat myself to some work on my Forearm Stand.

Most all of my yogi friends are runners. They run alone, in groups, in marathons and even in the mud. Myself, I have never really run. I feel self-conscious, especially outside.

But I long ago gave away my unused treadmill, even though it was great for hanging laundry, and so for this month I was outside in the evenings. And I would start off with a walk.

I'd put on my headphones and chat on the phone until I found myself up the street, through the park and out of the neighborhood. By the time I finished talking and turned around, the sun would be on its way down and so would I.

It's literally downhill all the way home, and that's when I'd pick up the pace. Running under the cover of darkness, I'd turn on the music and go. By the time I reached my house, I'd have that same feeling that comes over me at yoga in Savasana, or final resting pose. I'd feel energized, lifted and content.

This was new for me, being outside. Growing up, I danced a lot, and that was always indoors. In fact, I think those memories are some of what hooked me on yoga.

I passed along my dancing joy to my daughter, and all the while she was growing up, she danced, too. She especially loved to tap and did so all the way to college.

It was always hard to find a place for her to practice at home. Mostly, she would tap in the attic, and I'd mark the dates of her home performances on the attic's wooden floor while the family squeezed around to ooh and aah.

It wasn't long before she outgrew the attic, and my father made her a portable wooden floor. This we could put in any room, and on it she shuffled, step-ball-changed, brushed and flapped. There were more steps on that floor than anywhere else in the house.

In the years since, the portable floor has become one with the wall on the outside porch, leaning upright and gathering pollen and dust. When I got the news about my month with no yoga, I brought the floor in from outside and wiped away the intervening years. Once clean, I spread my mat overtop.

Each night after my walk-run, I'd come home to the mat on the tap board. I'd stretch into Paschimottanasana, or seated forward fold, and then into Baddha Konasana, or seated butterfly pose. And then, in my grandest goal of the month, I'd pop several times into Pincha Mayurasana, or Forearm Stand. With no weight on my hand, I did what I was missing the most, going upside down.

And like the family with their oohs and aahs, I'd set up my phone to snap some pictures of my inversions. And like the dates marked on the attic floor, I'd number those pictures with the number of days passed, creating an illustrative countdown to what I hoped would be the go-ahead to practice again.

It was different, though. There was no instructor telling me what to do next. There was no heated room, no group energy. I was in it on my own, and it was work to keep at bay the worries about whether I'd still have my practice by the month's end.

In discussions with my instructor, I asked whether she had ever taken time off from her practice.

Yes, she answered, *and I was stronger for it.*

At the time I thought she was talking about her body, how her rest had actually strengthened her muscles. But once I was in it, I realized she might have been talking about another kind of strength, the kind that is summoned when it's time to come up with a new game plan, when the one you've worked so hard to put together is no longer an option.

That was the kind of strength I needed to build, because who knew when such skills might have to be summoned again?

At the time, though, I just stayed the course, continuing to tape those photos of my numbered Forearm Stands to the refrigerator. I reckoned that would help get me to judgment day.

And after that I figured I'd just map out whatever plan was next, preferably one that found me back on the mat, perhaps with a new and different kind of strength than was there before.

Humbled

The barriers get in the way, but I see hope in every cloud, and I'm thankful ... I've got all that I'm allowed.

~ALL THAT I'M ALLOWED, ELTON JOHN

It was my first time back on the mat in a month.

My hand had been healing, and I had done my best to stay motivated, trying to walk and run and stretch. But by the end I really was just spending my time waiting to come back.

On the day I was cleared to practice, I thought I'd be so excited; but, as the day wore on, I became more and more out of sorts. By the time I got home from work, I was not sure I'd even go.

I knew by the end of my month's rest that I would lose some strength and flexibility; however, I did not think that I'd also lose some confidence. I couldn't believe I was considering giving myself another week at home.

I had to start again, literally. On the night that was to be my first practice back, I jumped in the shower, as if the day were just beginning, and did all the things I do to get ready in the morning, even though it was the evening.

Feeling better, I packed up my mat, hopped in the car, and drove downtown to a beautiful yoga studio with a big, open practice room. I parked the car, walked around the corner and there on the city sidewalk stood my yoga buddies!

I was so thrilled to see them, these people who have come to mean so much to me. Their hoots, hollers and hugs welcomed me warmly and boosted my confidence enough to make my way with them to the studio.

As we sat in the lounge, the others asked if I knew I'd have to hold back. No arm balances. No Crow. No jump backs.

What's left for me to do? I asked, knowing that I had to start slowly but only now realizing how much.

They had a quick answer for me: *The rest of your practice!*

I come to this class for the bandhas and the balances, so this advice gave me pause. But they quickly told me how injuries could force a focus on other parts of the practice, and they even demonstrated some modifications.

One yogi told me an injury had helped her learn to go from a seated position to a handstand. Another told me how an injury had improved her Forearm Stand.

Their collective support and encouragement gave my confidence another needed boost, and we placed our mats in this most special and spacious room. The high ceiling fans circulated a warm breeze that made its way in through the open French doors.

The practice began and we moved with the breeze. We moved and we moved and we moved.

And it was as if I were dining on a long overdue meal. I wanted to gobble up whatever was next. I wanted to clean my plate, and I realized how mistaken I'd been to think that I would be left hungry without the arm balances.

Each and every pose was work, and when it came time for Crow, I instead sat in a squat with my knees together in front of me. Turns out, my heels couldn't even touch the ground! Maybe they never could? A new challenge served up.

When it was time to jump back, I simply stepped back, happy to be able to have any weight on my hand in the first place. A big helping of gratitude.

And I waited out the Side Crows in a forward fold, my head no longer as close to my knees. A bite of humble pie.

We flowed through Warrior I's and II's, Side Angles, Half Moons and Triangles, and we reversed them, too. The sweat started early, and I savored each movement, my muscles getting a taste of what they had missed for a month.

Then the instructor brought us to Humble Warrior. With Warrior I feet, I bound my hands behind me and leaned forward, lifting them up and over my back.

And there, with my head bowed to the mat, I felt such a rush of emotion that I had to catch my breath, as if I had eaten too fast. I was overcome with everything the evening had brought me.

I was back in my seat at this abundant banquet where everything was within reach: my practice and my mat; the instructor and the room; my friends and their energy, support and camaraderie.

As usual, the practice was over in the blink of an eye, but I was sated and my muscles ached as if the practice was brand new.

On the way out, a fellow yogi asked how I felt, and I told her I felt everything! She understood what I was trying to say and said it so much better.

You mean it hurt so good!

Exactly! I said, knowing I had only whet my appetite and would be hungry again in no time.

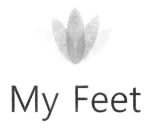

My Feet

My feet is my only carriage, so I got to push on through.

~NO WOMAN NO CRY, BOB MARLEY

I've never really given my feet a passing thought.

I have just taken them for granted, even with a father who was a practicing podiatrist for nearly 40 years.

But yoga has changed that. Now I understand what a precious commodity my feet are.

It's not that I have ever really ignored my feet. I keep them pedicured as a matter of course. And I decorate them with two toe rings, both representing something important to me.

When my daughter was little, she briefly attended a private school and could neither choose her wardrobe nor wear jewelry. On her last day, we each bought a toe ring representing a sort of freedom of expression that she had not been able to enjoy. A decade later, she sent me a new one from college, updating our freedom of expression and sending the message that it was something she still knew to seek.

A few years following, my son spent a college semester abroad in Australia. Far from home and knowing no one, he settled in fast, making another home away from home. During our visit with him, we stopped at an outdoor flea market where a jeweler fit me with a second toe ring. To me, it represented courage and an openness to new possibilities, both of which my son had demonstrated by taking such a journey.

More recently, though, I realized my feet were not so much pretty as they were precious when I found myself standing for three consecutive 12-hour days, working in the wrong shoes. Each evening, my feet cried with new blisters, and it actually hurt to walk. All I could think was that I would be out of commission for yoga.

On the first day, I wore beautiful new shoes with a platform and not too much of an incline. Six hours in, I realized my shoes had a time limit. Another six hours, and I hobbled into the house after driving home barefoot.

The hour was late, but I pampered my feet before sleep. I bathed them. I put cream on them. I rested them. I knew I had two more days of working like this before returning to yoga, and I could not imagine doing so.

The next day, I lowered my fashion standards and changed up my shoes. I put on what I considered not my best look, a more conservative pair with a lower heel. These shoes had a longer shelf life but still did not protect my feet from their fate. I went home that night with new blisters and again gave my feet the full spa treatment.

Finally, on the last of these three days, I slipped on my comfy flat shoes which had seen better days and were usually reserved for trips to the yoga studio. And that night I was relieved to find my feet sore but not too sad. And the next morning, I awoke pleased to realize they felt fine enough for yoga.

The first half of the practice is filled with several steps. It is a flow, all of which involves standing poses. We take many, many steps through Warrior I's and Warrior II's, Extended Side Angles, Reverse Side Angles and more. The rest of the practice takes place while we are seated, on our backs, and on our stomachs.

That morning I swung my feet over the side of the bed. The bed is tall and I am not, and my feet don't reach the ground. My painted toes with their rings hung overboard briefly before touching down with no pain.

My relief at my recovered feet made me realize that, even though yoga has taught me to appreciate my well-being on many levels, I'd never really appreciated how dependent I am on being physically able. And I'm sure there are other parts of me, besides my feet, that I've taken for granted, too.

I happily touched down that morning, grateful for the first time not only for all the steps that yoga has taught me, but also for the very simple fact that I could take them.

Speech

On a magic carpet ride, you don't know what we can see. Why don't you tell your dreams to me?

~MAGIC CARPET RIDE, STEPPENWOLF

It's said that our bodies can speak to us and, if we're listening, we can hear the whispers.

Mine speaks to me in the yoga studio as it did the other day at high volume, yelling at me when I again pulled what I discovered was my Quadratus Lumborum, a big name for a little muscle in my lower back. I had to roll up my mat and leave the practice early.

That night I booked an appointment with the miraculous masseuse who had once before fixed up the same sore muscle. Then I skipped my next yoga class in order to rest. Anxious to return but moving too fast, I attended a few more classes before realizing that my body just needed to be silent for a while. I gave it heat, ice, and pain relief, and then booked another massage.

I was off my regular practice schedule for two weeks and, oddly enough, I felt as if I had lost my voice. During this time, I found my mind busier than usual, and so I tried to put my story to paper, only to erase the words once they appeared.

I was missing my daily read, the story that is my practice with its usual beginning, middle and end.

The beginning of class usually starts off with some initial stretches and twists, allowing our bodies to yawn awake. This is when I have to consciously keep myself from chatting with my neighbor. I don't know why, but at this point I always want to talk.

Oddly enough, by the time we are flowing midway through, my mind quiets, and it's just my body talking. For me, this is the best part. Having never exercised before finding yoga, I'd never known what it was like to work out and sweat. It's an amazing feeling where nothing seems to matter but the movement.

The ending of class finds us down on our mats for some final stretches and twists. I never really want the flow to end, and when this time comes it's hard to wind down.

It seems the more energy I expend, the more I seem to have, and it's as if my body has so much more to say. So when I hurt my back and had to rest from yoga, it was kind of like being speechless. And I was afraid that once I returned I would not find the words.

While home resting my back, I was going through some archived emails and came upon one from my son's first week of a semester abroad in Australia. He has a wondrous way with the written word, and his email allowed me to virtually step into his newfound Aussie life. His narrative brought news of his apartment, his classes, his roommates, his new spot to eat and, of course, his neighborhood beach.

My son considers his time abroad as his most ideal. He worked out every day, ate fresh fish and vegetables in his oceanside town, had an easy course load, and basically for four months lived the Life of Riley.

To me, it was as if he was in a semester-long yoga class. It was a time, I believe, when his body, mind, and spirit all spoke the same language, a time when he found his best voice.

In many regards, yoga moves me in the same direction, where my body, mind and spirit all strive to occupy the same space; where all the words fit on the same page, and where I can find my voice in places where before I was silent.

I finally returned to class after hoping to have sufficiently rested my back. Gratefully, I found all the words still there, just waiting to be spoken.

Satisfaction

Scrambled eggs, toast and butter and a cup of coffee.

For me, this is a meal of satisfaction. Simple tastes, I know, but this is truly my most satisfying meal, and often it is my breakfast, lunch or dinner.

The other night, this was the meal on my mind as I landed in my first Downward Facing Dog in my evening yoga class.

In my inverted V, I was looking at the back of my mat, staring at my toes and realizing I had not eaten enough that day for the 90-minute practice. Far from being in a state of satisfaction, I was in what I call a state of *shaky hungry*, and I get in trouble with those who know me for being so.

Yoga has made me a more mindful eater, and I do my best to indulge in proteins and complex carbohydrates, vegetables and the like. I even stopped eating meat. Generally, I try to eat well, which takes some planning, especially a few hours before class, and I try to drink lots of water during the day.

So here I was at the beginning of class with the instructor urging us to let the day go, to clear our minds, to let everything dissolve on our mats. She was preparing to take us through a practice that would lead to satisfaction.

All the while, though, I was setting my imaginary table with an extensive mental menu.

We flowed through our first vinyasa, moving from an inverted V into a plank, down to a low push-up, through to an Upward Facing Dog and back again to Downward Facing Dog.

We were instructed to breathe so that, together with the breath and the flow, our minds would clear. But my mind was full because my stomach was not.

I felt like Dorothy in *The Wizard of Oz* when her house swirls through the tornado, and she looks out the window to see various images of her life pass by. But instead of resting on a bed in a flying house, I was on my mat in a baking hot studio. And instead of seeing Auntie Em go by, what I saw was a cheeseburger, which is not even part of my diet!

And in place of the nasty neighbor pedaling past on her bike, I pictured a piece of chocolate cake, the kind with the intense fudge icing that I like so much. There went my sashimi platter that I often pick up after yoga, not to mention the hot and satisfying eggplant empanada to which I also sometimes treat myself.

Next thing I knew, I was thinking about the times when I was little and the evenings my sister and brother and I got to watch *The Wizard of Oz*. An all-time favorite, it aired only one night a year. It would be a school night, a night when we were not allowed to watch television. But my folks would make an exception, and we would rush home from an afternoon of Hebrew school, plant ourselves in front of the television and have dinner in the den, topped off by popcorn. Big excitement!

Needless to say, I was not having a mindful practice. How *The Wizard of Oz* became part of it, I'm not quite sure. And I certainly wasn't adhering to what I had recently read in an article posted on another studio's website about the increased payoffs of mental engagement during exercise.

The article listed the following tips on how best to mentally engage in order to maximize a workout:

- Encourage yourself with internal dialogue.
- Pay attention to verbal cues from the instructor.
- Work your hardest so as not to think of anything else.
- Mix up your exercise routine so it takes concentration to follow.

It was obvious that shrimp and broccoli and sushi rolls did not make the cut of what to think about to maximize a workout. My poor preparation had included a scrambled egg breakfast, a light lunch of the same, and a cookie and coffee, all before one o'clock in the afternoon.

I wondered if I would leave the class early to go grocery shopping. At home, the cupboard was as bare as the contents of my belly.

Somehow, someway, I made it through the practice, albeit a bit more wobbly than usual. And I left the practice without my usual feeling of satisfaction; instead, I just felt relief for having made it through.

I went straight to the nearby Japanese restaurant where I'm a regular after yoga. The sushi chef made what he calls the *Pretty Girl Special*, a beautiful platter of salmon sashimi with vegetables.

This I followed with a trip to the grocery store, eating my favorite ice cream out of the pint on the way home.

Not very ladylike. Not very yogic. But very satisfying all the same.

Truth 11

Self-acceptance can be nurtured
when self-compassion is encouraged.

Sisters

You know I'll never be lonely. You're my only one, and I love the things that you do. You're my best friend.

~YOU'RE MY BEST FRIEND, QUEEN

The other night at yoga, we practiced with our eyes shut.

We moved without seeing for 75 minutes. Apparently, it was the night to focus on our Third Eye, the body's energy center for insight and intuition.

I myself am more focused on not falling. And I have to admit that I open my eyes a few times. The first time is to make sure I'm not the only one with eyes closed, which of course makes me the only one with eyes open. The second time is to check the pose. And a few more times, I have to say, is because I just can't help it!

Aside from that, I move deliberately through darkness with those around me, listening to the matching melodies of the instructor's voice and the music. Periodically, we sit back on our heels and bring our hands to forehead center for a look inside.

I wonder if anyone else has more than just themselves inside, because inside me, I've got some company!

My grandmother, Kate, and her sister, Ida, were thick as thieves. *Two bodies, one soul*, their mother would say. From the very beginning of their lives, they were on a journey together. Born in Russia, their father immigrated to the United States and sent for the rest of the family when they were only a few years old.

And, although my grandmother outlived her sister by many years, they paced the days of their lives alongside one another, always together. When it was time for Ida to go to kindergarten, she refused, saying she would wait until the next year when Kate would be old enough to join her. And when it was time for Ida to get married, she refused, saying she would wait until the time when her sister Kate would find someone, too.

So Kate and Ida, two best friends, married another set of two best friends, Max and Duvid (Do). They had matching engagement rings, a double wedding and a shared honeymoon.

My mother remembers my Aunt Ida and Uncle Do coming over every Sunday during her growing-up years. The sisters would put dinner in the oven and climb into bed for a lazy afternoon, talking until it was time to eat.

During the rest of the week the two spoke every day.

For some reason, since I've started practicing yoga, I've been thinking about these two sisters. I feel a kinship with them, and when I look inside I feel their presence.

When I was little, we saw them every Sunday, too. They were in charge of my siblings and me when my parents traveled, and they patiently watched the many shows my sister and I would perform. We sang songs and played Four Square. And best of all, my Aunt Ida let us toss *knaidles,* the Jewish version of dumplings, clear across her kitchen and into the pot.

And now, as an adult, these sisters are back with me, even recently appearing at one of the few meditation classes I've attended.

I was seated in a circle at a session led by a rabbi who's established a mindfulness center at his synagogue. The rabbi related a story from the week's Torah portion and discussed its mystical meanings that so closely relate to the Buddhist teachings of yoga, and then we closed our eyes for a few minutes' meditation.

Afterward, people volunteered the thoughts they had behind their eyes. I listened but didn't speak, because what had appeared behind my eyes was more of an image than a thought. What I saw inside was my Aunt Ida and my Buba Kate.

Somehow I didn't think it was strange, but at the time I wondered why they had appeared. Now, though, looking back, I realize I was sitting in that circle because I was seeking something soothing at a tumultuous time. And sitting there with my eyes closed seemed to help me find just that.

In the connection behind my eyes, the image of these sisters passed along some peace.

A while ago, to celebrate a milestone birthday, I received from my parents my mother's necklace, embedded with the matching diamonds from Ida and Kate's engagement rings. With permission, I dismantled the necklace into a pair of earrings to be shared among the generations in the family; the diamonds, like the sisters, a complete set.

My Aunt Ida was my mother's confidant, a strong woman who lived her life outward, making many connections and sharing in her sister's family when she herself could not have children. It's my guess that my Aunt Ida may have been my Buba Kate's safety net.

Kate lost her husband and, years later, lost Ida. And then she stayed on her own, living in a much more isolated way.

And now, these days, when I sit back for a look inside, I see in myself the opposite sides of each sister. I see the one who connects so easily with others, and I see the one who remains more so on her own.

I've been battling to reconcile these two opposites, but now I'm thinking that maybe it's okay they're both there, like two sisters with one soul. Maybe having both is like matching up two diamonds for a beautiful pair of heirloom earrings.

The class is over sooner than I realize. Practicing like this has taken all my concentration, and it takes a moment to reorient myself. Soon after, I wrap up my mat and thank the instructor, grateful for the chance to have closed my eyes and seen so much.

No Regrets

Don't worry. Don't be afraid. Every little thing's gonna be okay!

~GIVE LOVE, MC YOGI

Trust that all that was needed to be done was done. Everything is okay.

These are the yoga instructor's closing words. At the end of each practice, we roll into a fetal position and rest for a moment, eyes closed. And each time she says these words. They wash over almost 30 of us who are each resting separately on our mats but together with one another.

How is it that, at any age, it can be so reassuring to curl up in a fetal position and hear the words most of us heard as babies?

Everything is okay. Simple words that we all want to be certain are true.

In my yoga practice, when I am moving well, the poses come easily, and the positions meld one into another through seamless transitions. And everything is okay.

However, there can be times when my back acts up, making the vinyasas, or transitions, difficult. Once I even had to gather my courage to roll up my mat mid-practice and sidestep my way over about 10 people to leave the room and give my back a break. And there can be times when my balance is just completely off, making it difficult to stand in Eagle pose or keep the wobbles at bay in Half Moon.

During the difficult practices, it doesn't really seem like everything is okay. But if I am to believe the instructor, then I need to trust that all that is needed to be done has been done, whether or not I wobble or fall out of a pose. I'm not supposed to have any regrets in my practice. However it goes is how it goes.

I do my best to remember this lesson off the mat. If a situation finds me feeling a little off balance, or if the day starts off a little bit wobbly, then maybe that is okay. Maybe I don't have to always be moving well and transitioning seamlessly for everything to be okay.

I know I raised my children with this philosophy. I've taught them that, if something is to come to fruition, then either it will or it won't. As long as they do what's in their power and have a little faith, then whatever is the result is actually enough.

It is okay.

To trust for everything to be okay, though, takes more than a little faith. It takes compassion for oneself, which for me can sometimes be a challenge. I can look back in some instances and decide that, if only I had done things differently, then a different outcome would have magically appeared. In these imagined scenarios, of course, the magical outcome is always the one I desire.

The practice of yoga encourages me to take the instructor's words to heart and, with compassion, trust in myself that I have done all that needs to be done.

And that all is really okay.

Inversions

Okay, it's time to play with an inversion.

With these words, the yoga instructor declares recess to the class. It's my favorite part of the practice when we have about five minutes to go upside down before our final stretches.

Any kind of inversion will do, as long as our legs are above our hearts.

Some people are in Shoulder Stand, on their backs with their feet in the air and arms tucked under their hips for support. Some people rest their legs up the wall. Others are in a headstand or a handstand or even Forearm Stand, trying one and then another and stopping in between to chat.

When I practice yoga, I rarely look around the room. The music and the instruction put me in a sort of zone bound by the edges of my mat. There are times after the practice when someone approaches to comment on a pose, and I am always amazed that anyone was even watching. I assume everyone else is in his or her own zone, too.

What's different now, though, is that during the inversion segment, I seem to have started to step out of bounds, looking past my mat to the others in the room. These days, I seem to be keener on watching other people go upside down than on going upside down myself!

I do a few inversions, and then I sit back and look at those around me. The class attendance varies and often the room can be crowded. There is a lot to see and everyone is doing something different.

It sort of feels like cheating on my practice when I take the focus off myself to view the others, but still I sit back on my mat and look around at the differing ages and abilities, shapes and sizes, and ranges of form and grace.

Maybe it's not so yogic to look around, but I find that I do so without any judgment. More often it's just with wonder. I wonder how it is that I have come to embrace this practice and to share the room with all these people several times a week.

What if I never tried yoga? All these people would be here upside down without me! Would I even know what I was missing?

It briefly crosses my mind that while we might move in unison during the practice, we all have our own stories that brought us to the class and to the practice itself. And each person's story is as important as another's, and just as important as my own. I think this is what makes me able to regard my fellow yogis with only wonder and amazement.

My look-about is pretty brief. It lasts just long enough to give myself a break from the inversions and to ready myself for more.

I pop up into another handstand, grateful to have my story and to be upside down in the company of others who have theirs, too.

The Spill

Something inside is telling me that I've got your secret. Are you still listening?

~SUITE: JUDY BLUE EYES, CROSBY, STILLS & NASH

I'm a pretty careful person.

I'm a planner and a thinker and an organizer. I like things in their places, stacked and folded.

I'm not speaking necessarily of the parts of my life that can be seen, like my clothes and papers and such around the house. I'm talking more about the parts that can't be seen. These are the parts like most of us have that are naturally kept under wraps.

I have friends who can talk about anything. And they do, often to me. I think that's because they know I will make a neatly folded pile for them, too, and set it aside, undisturbed for safekeeping.

This is what I've done for myself over the past many years. It's just that I didn't really realize how tall my piles were getting and how many had sprouted. I didn't know they were taking up so much space and resting at their teeter points.

This is how I stepped into yoga, thinking I was just there to exercise and believing there was more than enough time to keep folding and more than enough room to keep stacking.

But there's something in yoga called a Mudra. It's an energetic seal, a process that leaves no room for clutter. The practice awakens lots of energy and clears things out, readying a new space to be sealed in the body.

A Mudra can be big or small. It can be performed with the entire body or even with just the hands. We seal that special space created by the practice by just placing our hands to our foreheads or by connecting two fingers. We lock and bind our bodies in many ways to do this, too.

I have to admit, though, that the result can sometimes be a mess. I think yoga just came into my life at a time when I didn't know I was about to burst.

Unbeknownst to me, yoga caused a big spill.

It messed up my way of organizing things and forced me to sift through some ridiculously old stuff. Much to my surprise, words have fallen out of my mouth, my own secrets no longer sealed. The contents of my piles have been strewn about, and there's no cleaning them up.

I've grappled with this state of affairs and have come to the conclusion that yoga is a practice of acceptance, and maybe that applies to the self, too. I'm thinking that maybe I'm supposed to accept all the parts of those piles that were so neatly tucked away.

The mere fact that they spilled should tell me something, that living so undercover keeps others from knowing me, and keeps me from knowing myself.

It was a few years into yoga before I learned about the Mudras. These seals are supposed to be healing.

Let's seal the practice, the instructor says when it comes time for the end. I used to just hear that, but now I get that.

And after so long, I finally understand what it means for the practice to create space. All that energy stirring things up, making room by sweeping away whatever it is that no longer serves us. And then we get to harness that new energy in a newly opened space by sealing it in with a Mudra.

For me, though, the difficult part is to let the wind blow inside and to not see the aftermath as any kind of wreckage. Because when we practice, whatever is uncovered is only us, and we are all deserving of love and care and healing.

This is what the practice honors. This is what the Mudra seals. And this is what that new space is for.

Pruning

You're gonna find, yes, you will, that you're beautiful as you feel.

~BEAUTIFUL, CAROLE KING

The other night, I heard a story about a man's life.

He told it in 10 minutes flat through a metaphor about his favorite tree. He was a generous and engaging speaker, conversational in tone and easy to hear. He used his Japanese maple as the metaphor, describing its canopy of leaves in the spring and summer, and its inner core of twisting branches bared in the winter.

He has had to learn how to tend the tree so that it lives year round. This involves cutting back the branches and, while the pruning often leaves scars, he explained that this is what facilitates the tree's growth in all sorts of new directions.

Yoga has sort of pruned me.

I had heard about this, that yoga peels back the layers, but I had never really believed it. I didn't even know I had any layers that needed peeling! And really, I began this practice for the exercise only.

Little did I know the practice would provide more than a glimpse of my inner core, and that I would get a full-on view of some of the scars found there. Somehow, each pose opens the door, helping me inside myself in a way I couldn't find before.

I think it was the backbends that did me in. They are supposed to be heart openers, and we do several variations of them, Wheel and Camel and Dancer and Locust and Bridge and Bow and more.

The heart shines through in each of these poses. It is physical but also apparently emotional and, although I am aware of the physicality while working through the poses, I am often surprised by any subsequent emotional effects.

The speaker displayed pictures of his Japanese maple, one from the spring with its canopy, and one from the winter without. Of course, the springtime photograph was lovely with its lush leaves, but there was even more beauty in the bareness of the winter one with the tree's dark and twisting branches still straining toward the sun.

Beautiful inside and out.

I have heard these words before, that I am beautiful inside and out. But when the pruning begins, and I am privy to the bareness inside, it can be a challenge to believe.

The speaker said that, at one point, a winter storm dumped a clump of snow on the leaves, and the tree broke before he had a chance to brush it away. He said he just fixed it up with what was handy - duct tape - making do with what he had on hand at the time.

Yoga has even more poses that open the door for a reveal inside. Along with the heart openers come the hip openers, including Pigeon and Lizard and Goddess and more.

The practice of yoga asks that we set an intention; however, mine was only ever to get fit, not to peel and reveal with the heart and the hip.

In the end, though, I guess what matters is that I grow from the inside out, even if I find myself twisting in a new direction. And if that's the case, then maybe I can be like this man's maple tree and head toward the sun.

Reflection

At yoga, I sometimes practice in front of mirrors.

For a while, I only practiced this way. So almost every day and often first thing in the morning, I'd be eye to eye with myself in front of floor-to-ceiling mirrors.

And because my mat was placed so near, I'd have a pretty close-up view. I'd see myself, then, like this, from head to toe, in a little outfit, hair back, and many times without much makeup.

Basically arriving at the yoga studio was like coming out of hiding. I'd be there on my mat with no armor, so to speak.

Seeing myself up close and personal on such a regular basis was quite enlightening. It made me see a clearer picture.

I've never considered myself vain, and I've never been one to primp throughout the day. After I'm dressed and ready to go in the morning, I rarely check the mirror again.

For much of the practice, I'd be pretty oblivious of my reflection. In fact, at one point, there was a photographer in the studio, and the instructor gave me some photos. It was a kick to see myself doing yoga, and I realized that, even though I practiced in front of the mirrors, I never really saw myself.

In many poses, we have to find our drishti, or focal point, to help us balance. This happens in Eagle and Dancer and Chair and more.

Look at a stare point, the instructor would say. *It can be your eyes or a point on the floor in front of you.*

Being in the front, I'd be forced to look in the mirror at my own eyes, and I was surprised to find it a bit disconcerting. I'd balance and my gaze would flit. I'd look from my reflection to that of the back windows. I'd look in the mirror at whatever else was over my shoulder, and I'd glance once more at my own eyes before looking aside again.

Why was this so weird for me?

I always thought I knew myself so well, but now I think the discomfort in seeing myself eye to eye tells me I may not have been as familiar as I once thought.

I couldn't seem to pass my own stare test.

If I were to be honest, I would say that looking into my own eyes presents a challenge to really, really see myself. And if it were easier to do, I would probably have an easier time letting others really see me, too.

Everyone loves you, Mom, my daughter tells me. She says I should see myself as others do.

But I know experiences can skew one's view, and I think that's what happened to me.

Yoga has made me stronger. It has given me muscles, for sure, but it has also given me the courage to see what broke so long ago. I had not really looked in years. It's been difficult to look at my eyes in the mirror because, when confronted with myself, I see those pieces, and I am critical.

Thankfully, yoga is also teaching me to have some compassion for myself and to build my strength from there.

At the end of each practice, we hold our hands in prayer in a seated position, bowing our heads to thank the teacher within. And I do so with gratitude because, through yoga, I am healing with some long overdue self-love.

·

Breathe

Warrior

Reset

Mentor

Silly

Embrace

Truth 12

Connections can be formed
when support is secured.

Breathe

We're one, but we're not the same. We get to carry each other.

~ONE, U2

In general, I'm a pretty private person.

I keep things close to the chest, and even when I share, I proceed with caution. I connect easily with others and have been trusted with many confidences, but it's only on the very rare occasion that I share mine.

The hitch for me is being okay with the natural flow of people who come in and out of my life. If I had my way, I'd keep most everyone who passed through, especially those with any of my confidences in tow.

The balance between connecting with ourselves and with others was the theme of one of my yoga classes, where the instructor told us that connections take practice. She encouraged us to use the practice to connect first with ourselves and then with others.

This is called a practice, the instructor said. *If you already knew everything, there would be nothing to practice.*

In yoga breathing is the key to connecting. Breathing takes us out of our minds and into our bodies, out of the stories in our heads and into the present. The breath helps the thoughts of yesterday and tomorrow drop away until we are left where we belong, in the moment where we are supposed to be.

We breathe through three vinyasas. A vinyasa is a set of three poses, and one travels through them on the breath. We exhale to a low push-up, then inhale to an Upward Facing Dog, and then exhale to a Downward Facing Dog.

The instructor reminds us that, although our practice is personal, we should not forget the others in the room.

She says, *Once you connect with yourself, you can connect to others.*

I can hear all of us breathing on the same beat, the class synchronized on its inhales and exhales.

Breathing is the basis of the yoga practice, and it takes practice to breathe. I guess, then, that the connections I find between the physical practice and the life lessons found therein should not surprise me. I have to breathe through both.

Maybe it's telling that sometimes the instructions to inhale or exhale often find me holding my breath while holding a pose.

It can be challenging to be truly connected with myself, to breathe into my life's moments both in and out of class. For a long time, I let myself hunker down, resisting opportunities to breathe. It was a safe place to be, but there was no flow, and it didn't get me anywhere but from one day to the next.

In this particular practice, we are inches from our neighbors, and the instructor encourages us to use our breath to connect to and inspire others in the room. She wants us to see our fellow practitioners as pillars, saying that we live and practice in and among others, and that connecting to ourselves gives us the trust to connect to others.

And while I'm usually oblivious to those around me during my practice, it's true that I can't help but benefit from the energy of those so near. So, in return, I breathe.

Breathing creates space in both the body and the mind. It makes room for connection. As I inhale and exhale, I think back to some recent advice where I was told to offer myself some space for life's missed or lost connections. This space is supposed to provide a cushion of care and protection from self-blame.

On a day following, I asked another instructor what else there was to learn. I had advanced through many of the poses, and I was looking for the next challenge. My practice was feeling stagnant.

For you, he said, *it would be the breath.*

Warrior

Don't be so hard on yourself. Those tears are for someone else.

~DON'T CRY, SEAL

We were standing in Warrior II, a pose that at one time had been my favorite.

My arms extend from front to back, my legs lunge forward, and my hips open to the side. At one time, I thought this pose was easy. Now, I beg to differ. It's almost 100 degrees. Sweat is dripping down every part of my body. The class is an army of warriors, and the instructor is our commander, pointing out minor adjustments to everyone in the room.

Move your front knee toward your pinky toe. Drop a little lower in your hips.

The instructor actually reaches behind my knee and pulls it forward to entice my hips to drop. It works.

Look past your front hand. Push your shoulders down. Don't forget to relax your jaw.

Each instruction is so minor, but every incremental shift feels so major. I am sweating Warrior II! Once all instructions are followed, we are supposed to just land there and be still, except, of course, for the breath. No matter what, we are supposed to breathe.

And just as I am wondering why we are doing this, why we have to remain so still for so long, the instructor issues a new command.

Be the bedrock!

She starts to speak about the strength of our foundation, how we are supposed to pull the energy up from our feet, which are pressed down firmly, and into our hips. Our base is supposed to be strong and steady.

Don't be the driftwood! she admonishes, before releasing us from the pose with the long awaited instruction to cartwheel it out.

I roll my back arm up and over my shoulder to meet my front arm and gratefully lower my body on an exhale before pressing upward and through my vinyasa.

I am the bedrock for many people in my life, and it has not been hard at all. I have not had to sweat it out, to say the least. It's been easy to be there for my children, my sister, my parents, my friends and my colleagues.

I am often told by others that I've helped them see their way clear. I've been told that I *envelop* people, and on a lark I visited a Vedic astrologer who told me I'm someone with whom others share their *shadow sides*, or secrets.

But even a piece of bedrock needs to lean on others sometimes, and this has taken me a long time to learn. For me, it's not so easy to reach out. To be honest, that is what I really sweat! And this is where I think I disagree with the instructor. I've learned that sometimes it's okay to be the driftwood.

For the first time I've reached out to others for support, and I have been the recipient of an overwhelming dose of wisdom, love and comfort. And I have to admit to a certain relief, even though at the time I sort of felt that doing so might be a negative, almost as if for me to flounder might be a bad thing. It's certainly not an easy thing, but maybe it's how one gets to the other side of something problematic.

One friend, a fellow warrior, really, sent me a message, almost giving me permission to drift.

She said, *Remember you must take care of yourself and those you love. It's okay to lose focus once in a while. That's all part of life, and it's all good as long as you can get up, brush yourself off and go forward.*

I call her a fellow warrior because she, too, has successfully come through some hardships and has seen her way clear to a good, strong place.

After our vinyasa, we move into Warrior I, a difficult pose with arms up by the ears, legs in a lunge but with hips forward this time.

Move your hands to your heart and spread out into Warrior II, the instructor says.

Our army follows its commander, who allows us the moment to touch our hearts in the transition between Warrior I and II.

I land again in Warrior II, sweating but feeling strong, moving between poses and excusing my heart its breaks in between.

Reset

Startin' over. Over, and over, and over, and over.

~(JUST LIKE) STARTING OVER, JOHN LENNON

When I was little our family was five around the table every night for dinner.

I really can't remember a time when we were not all there together. Dinner balanced out the day, and dinner was always balanced. Our plates were filled equally with a protein, a vegetable and a starch. One night was fish, another steak, another our favorite of meatballs, potatoes and peas.

Dinner was like a reset button on the day. Whatever the day was, it was shared around the table over an abundant spread. We served ourselves, and we had to finish everything on our plates.

These days, yoga serves as my dinner in this way, most recently in a hot class with the room heated to at least 95 degrees. Twenty minutes into the class, I was wondering if I would make too much of a scene if I rolled up my mat and left. It was tough. It was hot. It was not my usual practice. And it had barely begun. Plus, my mind was busy with things at work and at home. I was preoccupied.

In between instructions, the teacher spoke and after a while, between her words and the flow, my mind settled as my body dined on the poses.

Be here, she said. *Your practice will be whatever it is. What matters is that you showed up. So you might as well be present.*

Could she read my mind?

Your practice is like clearing your plate, she continued. *You get to come here and hit the reset button.*

She kept on talking, engaging our minds as we engaged our muscles. She told us about her young daughter, nervous to start the school year, fretting that the year would begin as the old one had ended, fearful that the June stories would be the September ones, too. Her child was too young to know that the summer often serves as a reset button.

This reminded me of my daughter at a similar age when she landed a spot in a sought-after private school. A lot of wonderful things came out of the years she spent there, but, ultimately, I moved her back to the public system. Everyone at the school balked, except for one mother whose daughter had actually just been accepted after two attempts at the application process.

Although we were taking opposite routes, she said to me, *There is never a problem re-evaluating and re-directing.*

I had not asked for these words, but they were generous all the same, and I've never forgotten them. This mother understood the value of resetting.

It occurs to me that I have had to hit the reset button many times in my life, and from a positive perspective doing so has been a useful tool.

One hour into the practice, I was feeling good, and we moved into Pigeon pose. Pigeon is a hip opener, and I've been told it's a pose that can release emotions that get stored there. I find this to be a difficult pose. My hips are often tight and, truth be told, I don't know how much I really believe about emotions being stored there. But this practice surprised me.

As usual, it was work to rest in Pigeon, and maybe the instructor saw me fidgeting. She came over and pressed my right hip to the floor with her right hand, and pressed upward on my back with her left. My body was flush with the floor, my hip opened more and, to my surprise, out popped a few tears. I was grateful to have my face toward the floor, my eyes closed and hidden from view. We moved to the other side, the left leg forward this time, and the instructor came back to repeat the press. A few more quiet tears.

I was reset.

The final half hour was filled with core work and stretches. With my mind no longer busy, I realized I had reached the end of class without beating a hasty retreat. For this day, my plate was cleared. I was at the dinner table again, the class my instant family, the practice my balanced meal.

Dessert was a sea of three *Oms,* our voices overlapping in the final serving of the day.

Mentor

Old, but I'm not that old. Young, but I'm not that bold.

~COUNTING STARS, ONE REPUBLIC

I'm learning from the other side at yoga.

I am relatively new to a nighttime practice not so close to home. And for this reason, most all of the yogis, save one or two, were strangers when I first arrived.

But the energy in the room seems to tie us together and, at the end of each practice, I often feel a sort of kinship with my classmates, even with those I still don't know.

In this class, half the room faces the other half. And now I've made some buddies on the other side. In particular, my drishti, or focal point, seems to land on a young lady three rows ahead in the first row that faces mine. She is upside down in a handstand for every vinyasa, and I'm hoping to advance my practice simply by osmosis.

One day on my way out, I couldn't help but exclaim to this young yogi about her practice. A few days later on my way in, she returned the compliment. Here I was admiring her, but there she was admiring me!

We started to chat and moved quickly to important topics like her handstands. I want those handstand vinyasas, away from the wall, and I asked her how it is that she's not afraid to go upside down, right in the middle of the room.

I'll help you, she offered. *I'll teach you how to fall.*

She spotted me, then, in a handstand, mid-room with no wall, and encouraged me to turn my hips and step out to stand up. It was almost like rounding-off in gymnastics or like the second half of a cartwheel. We did this a few times, and she sent me off to practice at home. Not once but twice after that, she offered to repeat the spot.

Here was someone offering help without my asking, offering only kindness and encouragement and even praise. Little did she know how much this heartened me.

Outside of yoga I find myself mostly in mentoring roles. I am a helper and often an advisor, as a mother, a sibling, a colleague, a friend.

Yoga puts me on the other side of the mentor, placing me in an unfamiliar role. And it feels kind of strange over there. At yoga, I'm the student. There, I look to others, students and teachers alike, for inspiration and how-to's.

And I'm surprised how much there is to learn, and how it's often from those younger. To me, it doesn't go unnoticed that someone half my age is imparting a life lesson. This young yogi is teaching me about fearlessness and courage. She is teaching me how to be brave enough to fall, even when I might be scared.

Not too long after, I was seated at the end of a practice that focused entirely on handstands. It was truly the most difficult yoga practice I'd ever had, and I loved it. Exhausted and with my upper arms already holding the memory of the practice, I awaited the closing words of the instructor. I had no idea that he had read my mind about how much older I was feeling that night than those around me.

It doesn't matter how old you are, he announced to everyone, *or how long you've been practicing. If you're alive, you're practicing.*

Apparently, how old we are doesn't seem to matter. Yoga is an equalizer. This might not be evident when walking by each other on the street, but once we are on the mat, it's really so easy to see.

This unexpected camaraderie at yoga has been a welcome surprise. More than once, I've looked around and wondered, *What if we all never met or, for that matter, what if I never met yoga?*

What, then, if I saw these yogis passing by outside, walking around, all grown up and dressed up and doing their days? Would it even occur to me that at night we could all be having fun inside, upside down in headstands and handstands like children of all ages?

The other day, it was time to practice our handstands. I planned to chicken out and face the wall at the back of my mat for support. I was still afraid to invert at the front of my mat, mid-room.

But right before I turned around, my young mentor on the other side caught my eye and gave me a nod. So instead of making the turn, I accepted her silent encouragement and changed my plan.

Bolstered by her confidence, I gathered my courage and faced front. I planted my hands below my shoulders and pulled in my core. Slowly, I lifted one leg and then the other as my body climbed toward the ceiling.

And to my own amazement, I made it up there safely, hanging upside down at the front of my mat without a wall, balancing on the faith of my young mentor from across the room.

Silly

Everyone is so helpful, everyone is so kind, on the road to Shambala.

~SHAMBALA, THREE DOG NIGHT

It's been a few years. A few years of handstands.

When I first started yoga, I would not go upside down. I knew I could do it, but it just felt so silly.

I'd often goof around with my children, and some years earlier, before even finding yoga, I had done a headstand on Skype for my daughter and her college roommates. So it's not that I was never silly. It's just that I was never so in public. And the yoga studio counted as being in public.

Then one day it was just my daughter and me in a private lesson. In my mind this was not public, so upside down I went.

And then almost every day thereafter I only wanted to be upside down. Headstands led to Forearm Stands, and Forearm Stands led to handstands. I could not get enough.

And now I can't remember what there ever was to feel so silly about.

Now I say who cares about being upside down in public? It didn't matter who was looking the other weekend in New York City on a crowded Sunday afternoon in Battery Park!

About a year and a half in, I got pretty good at the balance. With a wall close by, I could stay up and up and up in handstand, and I felt like a pro. But then I received some new instruction about how to go up in the first place. I was supposed to go up by using my bandhas, or my core. Kicking up was off the list. Being near the wall was off the list.

It was like starting brand new. And it felt a little silly to suddenly be back at

Square One, and I realized I was so far from whatever a pro might be that it had been silly to ever even think that could be measured.

In fact, one yogi videotaped the class so she could take it with her on her travels, and she captured one of my few handstands that had actually worked.

I placed my hands under my shoulders. I listened to the instructor tell us to shift forward, to not bend our legs, to claw the floor with our fingertips.

One try. Two tries. Three, and then four.

On the fourth try, I felt my hips stack and my core engage while I lifted one leg and then the other, ever so slowly, up and up and up from the floor to the ceiling! In my mind, I was up forever before standing to regroup and repeat.

But the camera doesn't lie.

My fellow yogi posted the clip of my handstand on YouTube, and I saw that I was up for all of five seconds. And my regrouping moment really just shows me unable to keep my amazement at bay as I stand up, not really knowing what to do with myself and quietly exclaiming *Yaaaaaaaahhhhhh!*

I learn best in a visual manner. I need to see things or draw them out in order to take them in. So I've started to watch my yogi friends who've become my teachers, and I've listened carefully as the instructor's words draw the picture of what I'm supposed to do.

And I'm literal, too. One instructor keeps talking about the shoulder girdle, but I've been confused as to what that is. Plus, when she says this, I keep picturing my grandmother in her blue dress. As a little girl, I knew a girdle was under there, and I was confused about that, too.

Another instructor talks about keeping my hands active, pressing into the fingertips if I think I'm going to fall over and pressing into the palms if I think I'm going to fold. He shows me, but I tell him I need bigger hands.

And then there's the fear factor. I've been told to play in the grass because there I'll have less fear, and I've been shown how best to fall down so as not to be so scared going up.

I've been told to integrate my shoulders, and it really helps to watch one of the yogis roll back her shoulders again and again as she demonstrates how this engages the upper body while inverting.

And now after a few years at handstands, I realize what might be one of the most important tips. Surprisingly, my arms had escaped the list of parts to address when tackling this pose!

Up until this point, I'd been busy keeping straight all the things I had learned about my shoulders, my hands, my back, my core, my legs, my hips, my feet and my fear. I hadn't thought about the need to keep my arms straight, too.

I look to the pictures of my son and me in our handstands in the grass in Battery Park. Arms straight and strong, he is on his way up. I have peaked with my arms bent, and I know I'm on my way down.

The other day I was contemplating skipping my evening yoga class before the instructor posted a picture on Facebook with a shout-out to her evening students. There she was in a handstand with her arms straight and strong.

I took one look and thought, *I'd be silly to skip this!*

And that night, I pulled my mat to the wall during the inversions. I placed my hands under my shoulders with one leg up and shifted my weight forward. And without further ado, I pushed my other leg off the ground, lifted my hips, integrated my shoulders and straightened my arms.

I pressed into a handstand without touching the wall, working my fingers and my palms.

And I was up and up and up!

I did it once, and I did it again. My grandmother's girdle didn't even enter my mind, and the instructor snapped a photo.

The only thing that shouldn't be in that photo, she later said, *is that wall.*

I took note but knew that the wall wasn't the only thing that had removed my fear. That night, I had gathered all the generous encouragement, advice and support that have come my way and gratefully locked up all of it in my core. And then I let it lift and secure me into my handstand and into the night and into the next day.

And there is nothing silly about that.

Embrace

Lean on me when you're not strong, and I'll be your friend.
I'll help you carry on.

~LEAN ON ME, BILL WITHERS

It's impossible to be alone at yoga, even if you walk in feeling that way.

It was a weekend morning, and I was getting myself together for class. On Saturdays and Sundays, I actually shower, wash my hair and put on a little makeup before going to yoga. It may sound strange to do all this before working out, but this is the morning routine that wakes me up.

I was like this in college, too, even when just studying. I would wake up, shower, dress and sit among my friends who would all be in their sweats.

My son calls me the Cal Ripken of getting ready for the day.

I arrive at the studio and wait for the class to start. I open my mat in my favorite spot, and slowly the others start to trickle in.

I love seeing everyone, and a few people come over to chat and catch up. Some are young adults, the ages of my children, some are closer to my age, and many are in between. Yoga has introduced me to so many new people. I didn't know that practicing would make me part of any kind of community.

In general, I have never considered myself a joiner. I've always had lots of people around me, but I was never a committee-type person, nor did I ever belong to one particular group over another. Growing up, I had friends in and among all sorts of groups.

That being said, I would not call myself a loner either, but I do admit to a certain aversion to being pigeonholed in any way.

Our class begins, and the flow slowly builds as does the energy. The instructor allows for progressions in each pose, and this gives us a chance to do our own things. And that works for me, because even as part of a group there remains a part of me that can be more comfortable on my own.

Before yoga, I had found myself laying low. My trust levels had pretty much shrunk the size of my community, and I was content in this manner for a long time.

After my children left for college, I ventured out and got a job. Working made me suddenly part of a very large and global community, and I've come to know so many of my colleagues well. It's been a surprise to find that being connected with so many others is what I like most about my job.

Then I found yoga, and I became part of yet another community.

Some days, though, I can feel myself falling back into my old ways, raising the guard gates and hunkering down a bit. And those are the days when I make sure to keep my office door open, and when I make sure to get myself to yoga.

And so it is that I find myself practicing among others, individuals on our mats, doing our own things but doing them together. We follow the same instructions but progress in different increments. We move in the same motions, but do so in different styles and with different degrees of grace. Yet we are all one unit, and the appeal of the group's energy sweeps me along with the others.

I get into my own zone as I move through the poses but, lately, near the end, I've been looking around. On this day, we are given a few moments of self-practice. I do a few handstands followed by a few seated forward folds, and in between each I look around.

It's strange, but at this point I identify with each and every person in the room, those I know and those I don't. It's just impossible to be on guard when moving like this, and it's as if the efforts to balance and twist and rise and fold have exposed us all to each other.

Here I recognize everyone, and I feel suddenly tied to these kindred spirits. And, although I know we all stepped in for different reasons, it's as if our reasons are now all the same as we are to each other.

And I wish I could let everyone in this room know that the motion of their movements provide me with an embrace of energy that feels as safe and sound as someone's arms around me.

At the end of the practice, we lie down, and I settle into the protective power of this group's silence. Several moments later, the instructor has us roll to the right and rise to a tall, seated position with our hands draped over our knees. We are told to be grateful for our bodies, for the clarity of our minds, and for being able to practice.

Eyes closed, I inhale deeply with the others.

And then the class exhales on the same beat, sharing its breath in a hushed but audible whisper. And in one quick *whoosh*, it's as if I am part of some big secret shared by everyone in the room, and I am suddenly and surprisingly so very moved.

The guard gates have lowered, and I am flooded with immense gratitude for everyone around me, for it's their very presence that has helped me find something I had not even known I was missing.

Truth 13

Balance can be established
when the choice to let go is embraced.

Swimming

Rock me on the water. Sister, will you soothe my fevered brow? Yeah, rock me on the water, then maybe I'll remember, maybe I'll remember how.

~ROCK ME ON THE WATER, JACKSON BROWNE

One night, I was in a yoga class that took place in what I can only describe as *The Twilight Zone*.

I call it *The Twilight Zone* because I literally had no sense of time during the practice. I was so incredibly immersed in the movements that the end snuck up on me, and I only knew it was that time because the instructor dimmed the lights.

We start the practice at the top of our mats, the usual place to start. We press our feet down and lift our toes up, and we're instructed to extend our arms up and around and back into place, alternating first one and then the other until the room is like a pool of backstroking yogis.

And even though we are swimming, the instructor asks us to root down into the earth, to press into our feet as if we are instead on dry land, and to lift our toes and glide slowly as if we have many more miles to go. For 75 minutes, we swim these miles, pressing and breathing, always breathing, and coming to a stop only to feel the earth beneath our imaginary pool.

The flow lifts us from the floor to our feet and lowers us again. It's hard to recall how we get where we're going, only that we seem to continue to rise from the floor, coming up for air in this way.

We do a lot on each side, working the lunge and the twist and the balance and more. And I'm glad no one can hear me silently call out, *Come on, come on, come on!* when my quads can barely swim another lap on the mat.

This practice is sort of mesmerizing. We touch down on the mat only to rise up again, and two or three times the instructor talks about the earth, asking us to feel it through the floor, all the way down to the ground.

And I imagine it solid underneath, even though we are fluid above. And I think it must be like this for everyone else in *The Twilight Zone*, too.

When it comes time for Savasana, or final resting pose, I lie there as the music plays. The piece is instrumental, and I hear a violin and think to myself to ask the instructor for the name of the song, so I can listen to it again at home. And I wish I were more relaxed, because I think I'm not.

The violin plays, and I hear in the music the same balance I find in this practice. It is steady and grounding but also fluid and flowing.

Before I know it, I am in a deep, deep rest, after all.

It seems that, in *The Twilight Zone*, it's just a trick to think I'm not relaxed. In fact, I'm so flat out that I can feel the earth beneath my mat, even though we are one flight up from the street. And so I lie there with the others, like a swimmer collapsed from swimming as far as she can go.

It's quiet, and the instructor walks around the room, reassuring this one and that one with the gentlest of adjustments. I can hear his footsteps as he makes his rounds.

And it's then that it's quiet enough, for the first time in a week, for some thoughts that have been too overwhelming to think. It had been that long since some very sad news that I hadn't yet let surface.

But in *The Twilight Zone*, time is suspended in the balance between effort and rest. The mat is solid, and the room is safe, and there's a peace that makes it okay for these thoughts to finally appear without fear.

And then it's over in a blink, and I can't even remember the closing except for the three Oms, only one of which I can do because it takes a few moments to collect myself and transition out of the zone.

But once I'm out, I'm out. And the lights are on and we are back and now there's talk of what to eat. And so I get dressed and ready to leave but first take a quick look around, just to double check.

Everything is the same as when I arrived; everything except, that is, for me. And there is no pool. There never was, even though I swam for miles.

Yin Yang

Something's lost, but something's gained, in livin' every day.

--BOTH SIDES NOW, JONI MITCHELL

As a kid, my goal in life was to grow up to be a hippie.

When I was little I had a pair of denim-colored Keds. They were too cool for words, and I made them even cooler by tattooing them with my pen and ink drawings: peace and love signs, flower power, Kilroy was here, and the Yin Yang symbol.

I never really knew what the Yin Yang symbol meant, but I would draw it all the same. At the time, I thought it had something to do with infinity, but as I grew older, I realized it had more to do with opposites.

Today I've learned that Yin and Yang are actually two opposing yet complementary aspects of the self that make up a person's vital energy, or life force, otherwise known as Qi. According to Traditional Chinese Medicine, Yin is the quiet, passive energy found in each individual, and Yang is the opposite energy, active and heated.

The practice of yoga seeks to balance both in an effort to increase every aspect of a person's health, including physical, mental, emotional and spiritual well-being.

Once I started practicing yoga, I came to understand even more about Yin and Yang and about how they exemplify duality, and this was further impressed upon me during a practice.

We are in Tree pose. Standing on one leg, I bend the other at the knee so that my foot rests on my opposite inner thigh. I place my hands in prayer and find stillness, anchored by my stare point, or drishti.

After holding the pose for a bit, I interlace my fingers and lift my arms, my eyes following their rise, all the while still standing on one leg. My torso tilts back, and I look for the wall behind me, bending back and back and back.

Stand strong, the instructor says. *Don't be concerned about instability. After all, instability is only the opportunity for stability.*

Wobbling on my left foot, I listen intently and have a sudden understanding. Instead of thinking about how I can't hold the balance, I think about the opportunity to do so, and my body calms. I root into my standing leg with my hands raised high, and I become still.

I find the Yin and the Yang.

The Yin Yang symbol is typically black and white with two opposite shapes fitted neatly together. It's an illustration of the concept that a positive cannot exist without a negative, and that both, when combined, make up a whole. This harmony of opposites is a concept unveiled in a portion of the second verse of the ancient, classic Chinese text, The Book of Tao:

> *Being and non-being create each other.*
> *Difficult and easy support each other.*
> *Long and short define each other.*
> *High and low depend on each other.*
> *Before and after follow each other.*

This idea of the negative giving rise to the positive seems so simple, but the reality of such situations is not always easy. As with the yoga poses, it can take work to find the balance, but understanding this relationship of opposites can sometimes be the light at the end of the tunnel. It's even what makes me able to stand on one leg in Tree pose.

We switch standing legs, and I bring my other foot to the inside of my other thigh. My hands return to prayer, and I find my focal point once more.

My sudden understanding tells me that my almost falling over in Tree pose is really just an opportunity to stand up straight, strong and balanced, so I interlace my fingers again and reach my hands over my head while rooting down in my standing leg, this time on the right side. The opposite movements actually facilitate my balance, and I'm able to relax into it.

In yoga, a lot happens through enacting opposite forces simultaneously. In Tree pose, the pose I'm in, one leg presses down and straight while the other is up and bent. The arms stretch upward while the shoulders press downward. In handstand, the palms press the floor while the legs lift to the ceiling. In arm balances, the torso tilts forward while the hips tilt back.

It seems that the yoga poses are the physical manifestations of the second verse of the Book of Tao! Who knew?

Standing there, I realize that the essence of Yin and Yang, the second verse of Tao, and yoga itself are all really just about acceptance. It's about grasping both sides of something in order to have an appreciation for anything.

And therein lies the balance in just about everything, which is not such a bad lesson to learn while hanging out in a tree.

Adaptation

Changes in latitudes, changes in attitudes, nothing remains quite the same.

~CHANGES IN LATITUDES, CHANGES IN ATTITUDES, JIMMY BUFFET

At first I fit yoga into my life. Now I fit my life into yoga.

Once upon a time, I never even did yoga. That time is hard to imagine now. What did I do before? I fill so much of my time with yoga that there's hardly any leisure time left in a day, and I wonder what filled it until now.

Change is challenging for me and so taking up something like yoga, and doing it as frequently as I do, is something I would never have anticipated. I usually like to do the same thing I've always done, even if now I can't remember what exactly that was.

I am a creature of habit, as my son likes to point out. I find a restaurant I love, and it's the only place I want to go. I'm at a job where lots of people come and go, but I tease everyone that I will be the last one standing. I'm the only one of my siblings who has remained local and, in fact, I raised my children right down the street from where I grew up.

Nothing stays the same, Mom, my daughter tells me.

She already knows this as a young adult, but I've learned this much later. And I'm not sure how this is so, because not much has ever been status quo.

At yoga, I've learned that we have a front body and a back body. I never knew about this until I was instructed to breathe into my back body. Even though I might have been asking the obvious, I had to be shown where it was, because I didn't even know I had one. The part I breathe into is behind my heart, and when I breathe in this direction, I can expand the area on my back between my shoulders. I can do the opposite, too, and breathe into my front body, filling my lungs and lifting my heart in this way.

I just have to know in which direction, and then all I have to do is breathe.

How else to adapt to change? None of us can remain the same, and I don't think we're supposed to, either. I used to think the goal was to get settled into whatever the most settled place would be, but now I know different. Even my practice changes, from where I practice, to how I practice, to when I practice. Change happens and I think, while not always easy, it's best to do as I do in the practice and go with the flow. It's the only way to stay in the game.

It's the only way forward.

So now what I do is return my daughter's wisdom, and when she wants to know what's next, I reassure her with my own experience that it's not always necessary to know. All that's needed is to know that something is next, and whatever that is can be discovered upon arrival.

We were in Pigeon pose the other day, and I lay there in a heap after an hour of practice. I welcomed the rest, and I breathed into my back body. This is a pose in which we are encouraged to let go, and if the instructor says something at this point, it's usually along those lines.

Let go of something, he said. *Only you know what that is.*

Then he made a few suggestions, one of which caused me to raise my head from my heap.

Maybe you have a 40-year plan that you have to let go, even if you don't know what's next.

I think he was talking to me! Just becoming a yogi was a big change, and if I think about it, that transformation should prove to me that I'm able to adapt to other changes, too. It just takes me a little while to settle into something new as I have a tendency to look behind more than I do ahead.

Life can only be understood backwards; but it must be lived forwards.

These are not the words of the yoga instructor; rather, they are those of the Danish philosopher and theologian, Soren Kierkegaard. I'm guessing that he knew he had a front and back body, too. He wrote these words in the 1800s, but I find them to be true today as I do my best to follow them, so I can move my practice forward and move myself forward, too.

Half Moon

*May the good Lord be with you down every road you roam, and may sunshine
and happiness surround you when you're far from home.*

~FOREVER YOUNG, ROD STEWART

I'm not sure how this connection came to be, but the only way for me to balance
in the yoga pose of Half Moon is to visualize my son standing at the far end of
the studio.

Sometimes he is in his tennis whites like he was during his school years.
Sometimes he is in his dress clothes like he is now at his job.

Somehow, *seeing* him enables me to maintain my footing in the pose.

Seeing my son has always seemed to ground me. As a young adult, he has
lived away from home for several years, first in college and then at work. These
days, I only get to see him for brief stints, but those short times seem to set me
right, even when nothing is wrong.

I find Half Moon to be one of the most challenging yoga poses, and I have
spent a long while trying to perfect it. I'm still not there yet. I have to make every
effort to ground myself in order to balance and hold the pose.

Half Moon involves tilting the body forward on one leg and lifting the other
so that it's parallel to the ground. Hips and heart are open so they face the side
with arms spread wide, one to the floor and one to the sky. It's almost like taking
the shape of a plane, tilted completely sideways. Energy is supposed to spark in
every direction, and only one foot serves as grounding.

Most difficult of all is shifting my vision upward. In order to help raise my
vision while in the pose, I'm told to look at a far point in the studio. This helps me
look to the side that my body is facing, rather than down to the floor, although I'm

still not at the point where I can look to the hand that's raised to the ceiling.

The most amazing thing, though, is that when I look to that distant point, an image of my son appears in my mind. I automatically relax, and I feel a sense of grounding. It's then that I become still and find the balance with a strong current of energy flowing down my standing leg.

So now I call my son and say, *I saw you at practice! Today, you were in your gray suit with your briefcase over your shoulder.*

He takes this in stride, knowing his mother as he does. *Oh yeah?* he says, and goes on with whatever other topic he wants to discuss.

At one point, I paid him a visit to help him move from one apartment to another. On the early evening flight home, I looked out the plane's window and, at a far point in the sky, I saw the half moon.

The sight made me think of him, and even though I was up in the air, the ground did not feel so very far away. And neither did he.

Music

Certain songs carry me back.

Without a second thought, a song can make me remember a time, a place, a person, a feeling.

Music measures out segments of time long since forgotten and brings memories to mind in an instant. It has the power to heal, bringing a sense of balance with its beat and smoothing out a day in this way.

I think music is what got me hooked on yoga in the first place.

Not every practice has music, but I was fortunate enough to start with one that was somehow plugged into my playlist: Elton John, Van Morrison, Bob Marley, Eric Clapton, The Beatles, Seal, and more.

I have always loved music since I was young, and I've never really started a day without it. Like most of us, I seem to have a soundtrack that marks time throughout my childhood and into my adulthood.

In elementary school, I'd ride around with my transistor radio in the basket of my bicycle and spend hours drawing my album covers. I'd wake up to music every morning on my clock radio, and every night I'd play records on my stereo, a gift from my parents for my 11th birthday.

My first loves were Michael Jackson and Donny Osmond, both of whom I plastered on my walls before graduating to David Cassidy, whose picture I proudly carried on my lunchbox.

In one of my yoga classes, one song played, and I called out, *fifth grade!*

Led Zeppelin, The Who, Queen and Peter Frampton formed the backdrop to my middle school years and boys and dances, and songs from Chicago, Boston, Fleetwood Mac and the Eagles are forever embedded in my brain from my time on my high school dance squad.

Cat Stevens and Jimmy Buffet joined me at the beach during my college years; Diana Ross was the envy of all my sorority sisters, and I remember exactly where I was when Michael Jackson did his moonwalk. There was never a time when we readied ourselves to go out without Earth, Wind & Fire or the Commodores.

My children grew up listening to so much of my music, and I listened to so much of theirs. My son had his tonsils out in second grade, and we were in the house for a solid week during his recovery with Hootie and the Blowfish, every day for seven days straight. We called Van Morrison our *company music,* and played it every time we had guests for dinner. It was such a staple that I sent my daughter off to college with the soundtrack in case she was homesick.

I spent hours listening to music with my children while doing arts and crafts at the kitchen table during what would be multi-day projects. And to this day, Paul Simon's Graceland track is forever linked to my daughter's first business order, when we played it repeatedly while beading 90 necklaces by lantern light during a storm when the power went out.

And I still make my kids crazy with 20-dollar bets to see if they can guess the artist playing on the radio and even made one such bet with my daughter during our first private yoga session, when *Into the Mystic* came on by Van Morrison.

My son seems to have my same love of music but has a playlist 100 times longer than mine. I often call to tell him what song is on the radio, and he sends me names of songs and singers he thinks I might like.

Check out Michael Franti, one such text reads. Already familiar, I just text back the singer's words, *Say Hey, I Love You!*

And when Michael Jackson died, I was overcome with a surprising sadness, because it was larger for me than just losing him. He had lost me for a while, but once he was gone, I returned, buying up a bunch of his music. Somehow, I felt as if a part of my history was gone, and I wanted it back.

At yoga, the personalities of many classes are reflected in the playlists. The music helps set the tone of a practice, creating an atmosphere that reflects the instructor's energy and helps us build our own.

At the beginning of class, the instructor turns on the music and announces the opening pose. The other day, it was Child's pose. I placed my knees on either side of the mat and put my forehead down, stretching my arms forward and dropping my heart. The lights lowered, and the music began to play.

I can't really explain it further, but my mind instantly settled as the music filled the room.

And then I did what I always do. I inhaled deeply and let it fill me, too.

My Son

Beautiful, beautiful, beautiful, beautiful boy ...
... Before you cross the street, take my hand.

~BEAUTIFUL BOY (DARLING BOY), JOHN LENNON

I've learned that we never stop growing up, but I have a son who I keep thinking is all grown up.

Or so it seems to me.

I guess I think he is all grown up because it's hard for me to find anything more that I can still do for him or that he needs me still to do. As a young adult, he is self-supporting, living and working in another city.

When he was little, I'd hold his hand, buy his clothes, pack his lunch, play endless catch, sit on the sporting sidelines, keep him dry in the rain, and tuck him in at night. Now he does all that and more on his own, and I'm certainly not the one tucking him in at night.

When he was born I felt an immediate kinship, as if on the inside he was me and I was him, a symbiosis from day one. And it's like he knew this, too. As a baby, I would hold him and pat his back, and his little hand would pat my back right back as if to say, *I know, Ma.*

As a single mom raising this boy, I learned so much about myself. I found myself in this boy who would color and draw and then oil his baseball glove and break it in each night under his mattress; who would lay his head on my shoulder and then put on his hockey gear and skates; who would tell me he loved me but make me promise to lay low on the soccer sidelines; who would give me play-by-plays of tennis matches but ask me to wait in the car at practice; who would blast his music but still listen to mine.

As he grew up, I had to learn how to make space to respect his, so we could remain simpatico, so I could still come along for the ride that is his life.

It did not surprise me that soon after I took up yoga, he did, too, first in college to fulfill some credits and then more so as he started to work. And now when I visit him or he comes home, it's what we do.

The other day, we placed our mats alongside each other to practice at a new studio. Here the instructor played the music at an extra high volume every time we held a pose or worked a handstand. And each time it would be one of my favorite tunes from way back when, and my son would look over at me and grin and nod, *I know, Ma.*

And even though he is what I consider all grown up, he doesn't mind my reaching out to pat him in the middle of the practice, and sometimes he even pats me right back.

We do yoga. We get juice. We go to lunch. We even shop. He holds my hand as he walks me around the city from here to there throughout the day. And later I hear from his sister that he loves when I visit, because he says I fold right into whatever it is they do.

And I'm grateful for this, for the closeness and for the space that makes it possible.

And now I am surprised to see myself again in this grown-up young man. We have pictures from these recent days where I can see myself in him, although he looks like his father and his uncle. I am somehow appearing in this young man, and not just in pictures but in how we think, and in what we say, sometimes in the same words, and at the same time.

When our practice is over, we sit up and together we say, *Namaste.* And I am filled with such gratefulness to have practiced with my boy, feeling so blessed that he is there, and that I'm still able to give him a pat and get one back.

The next day, he invites me to an appointment. We are to meet there but it's raining, and he texts me that he'll pick me up with the umbrella. And I realize that, this day, he's the one keeping me dry in the rain.

Before this trip, my son was home for a visit. He looked around at several things from years past and said that some of it made him feel bad. As with everyone, there are things left behind that would rather be forgotten. I know this is true of me; how can it not be true for him?

In yoga, one of the things we are taught is that it's okay to let go, that we don't have to hang on to everything that brought us to where we are now. So I make a promise that on his next visit home we will purge the old stuff, and lighten the load.

It made me think back to the end of a practice months earlier. I had turned my mat to the wall, facing a new direction by the end of class. It was hot. I was wrung out. The practice had done its magic before the instructor added some of his own.

Letting go is not a loss, the instructor said, his words like a wand sweeping across the room. I felt him grant me the same permission I wanted to grant my son.

It's not a lessening. Letting go, he said, *actually makes room for abundance.*

This winter my son went snowboarding, an annual activity that kind of scares me. On some such trips, I ask him to please just send a signal that he's breathing. I figure that makes for space because I don't need a phone call; instead, just a short text will do.

This time, the message reads: *Alive and well,* and it comes with a picture. He is in a headstand atop a snowy mountain, sending a signal loud and clear.

He might as well have just sent the words, *I know, Ma.*

Truth 14

What's broken can be repaired
when the spirit is energized.

Confessions

There is a crack, a crack in everything. That's how the light gets in.

~ANTHEM, LEONARD COHEN

We all carry secrets, some large and some small.

The small ones are universal. They are the everyday thoughts we keep to ourselves as we walk around doing whatever it is that we do.

And what I do almost every day of the week is yoga. For the most part, the practice clears my head. Whatever is on my mind seems to leave through the music and the movement. After one such practice, a fellow yogi walked up to me to compliment my poses.

How long have you been doing yoga? he asked.

A timely question, as the anniversary of my start was the very next week, and I told him so.

Well, he said, *I just watch your poses, and I'm not sure I'm ever going to get there.*

That would have been a good time to reveal some of my inner yoga thoughts; instead, I just thanked him.

He introduced himself and explained that he wasn't sure whether he'd ever be able to advance in the way he saw my practice, so in return I did make the small confession that when I started, I knew nothing.

What I did not tell him were my yoga secrets.

The first of which is how very self-conscious and out of my league I felt at the beginning. I had never before exercised, and I found myself, especially on certain days, in a class of mostly women with what I saw as intimidating arm muscles. They all seemed younger and looked as if they had worked out for most of their lives, which no doubt they had.

I instead just told him that when I first arrived at yoga, I was extremely cautious of my back, and that I was resistant to trying a lot of poses, especially the backbends.

Another fact I kept under wraps was that I was sort of inhibited at the beginning. And yoga pretty much demands the dismissal of inhibition. We put our bottoms in the air, lift our legs and open our hips, squat down with our knees apart, and lean back and open our chests to the sky.

It was almost all too much, plus the instructor would come by and adjust us.

And that was another thing I kept to myself. Even more than being intimidated or inhibited was the fact that I was someone who most likely had her guard up higher than anyone around. I was and still am very cautious of anyone who gets close. To say the least, having someone approach to move my arm or tilt my shoulder or adjust my hip was not really in my comfort zone.

Instead, I just told this new yogi that, in the beginning, I was afraid to try a lot of the poses, too.

It is difficult to explain what yoga has done for me, so I don't really say much about that. And my strategy from the beginning has been to just keep coming back. And I have been on a ride ever since.

Very, very slowly, I eased my way into the practice, letting go of intimidation, letting go of inhibition, and letting go of my guard. Yoga sort of broke me open. And that is really how I started to advance.

But I do not say any of this to the morning yogi speaking with me. Instead, I just tell him not to be afraid to try the poses, even if he thinks he can't do them. I tell him that one day he will get it, and then his body will always remember it.

His response was to tell me that I was inspiring.

I said a quick thanks and got ready to leave, thinking he should only know what I say to myself during some parts of the practice. The music and the movement might clear my mind for the most part, but not for all the parts.

When it's time for Dancer pose, a heart opener and standing backbend, I say to myself, *Oh, no, Dancer!* And when it's time for Lizard pose, a hip opener into which I am learning to take an inversion, I say to myself, *Oh, no, Lizard!*

These openers are rough in more ways than one. It is sometimes hard to open if there are some broken parts. However, there is a theory of sorts about how these breaks create the spaces through which the light gets in.

So maybe it is good to be broken open, after all, even if it means dreading Dancer and Lizard, because through yoga I've created some such openings. And this has let in some light to free me from the intimidation, inhibition and guardedness with which I arrived.

And this freedom has been very healing.

Still, I don't say a word about this to my fellow yogi. Some things are better left unsaid. And besides, he is only at the beginning of his yoga ride, so there is still time for his light to shine through, too.

Open

And when the rain falls down, you know the flowers gonna bloom. And when the hard times come, you know the teacher's in the room.

~HAVE A LITTLE FAITH, MICHAEL FRANTI & SPEARHEAD

One of the surprising things that yoga has taught me is that physical exertion has effects that go beyond the body.

It seems to offer an unexpected openness and peacefulness, allowing me to hear things I think I might otherwise miss.

I once had a lesson on backbends. It was the start of my goal to drop into a backbend from a standing position. With hands at heart center, I want to be able to lean back and, oh so slowly, land my hands on the mat behind me.

I am not sure why. I cannot explain this.

The lesson begins with the instructor stretching out my back and, in the hour that follows, we do all sorts of poses that bend the back: Camel, Wheel, and even some acro yoga where I hang in a backbend from the instructor's shoulders. But even though I catch a glimpse of my goal with some assists in backbends from standing, the lesson ends with the knowledge that it would be quite some time before I'd be doing this on my own.

I leave and arrive home so relaxed that I nap in what feels like a twilight sleep. This peaceful feeling lasts until I arrive at class the next day.

What did you do to me? I asked the instructor.

We opened you up, he answered.

Not long after, I found myself in a hot yoga class where we were instructed through many sets of backbends, both Bridges and Wheels. I was two-thirds of the way into the 90-minute class. The heat was intense and so was the practice. Sweat dripped into puddles across my mat as never before, forming a true body of water over which my Bridge spanned.

In this class, for the first Bridge, the instructor counts backward from five. On my back, I press my feet into the ground and hoist my hips, binding my hands and pressing them into the ground, too. I hold there and stare at my belly button for five, four, three, two, one.

Then follows a moment of rest, while we decide whether to repeat the count in another Bridge or move instead into Wheel. Wheel is just another name for a backbend, and I find myself lying there, floating in my puddle while the instructor encourages us to place our hands by our ears and set up for the ultimate choice of a backbend.

Come on! This is what you came for! Be here!

I press into my hands and feet and lift my hips to the sky for a full backbend.

This time I can't see my belly button. It is looking at the ceiling, and I am looking at the back wall, my arms fully extended, my shoulders off the ground, and my heart shining through in Wheel.

Five, four, three, two, one. Splash!

I gratefully submerge into the cooler temperature of my puddle and fantasize about remaining afloat while the rest of the class completes the sequence without me.

Set your hands. Everybody this time! Come on up into Wheel!

This is so different from my other classes where the temperature is not as high, where we only do one or two Bridges or Wheels, where the counts don't begin in the third round at 10, followed by another at 15!

What is interesting here, though, is that as I try to hold the backbend for the high count, the instructor stops counting altogether and tells us she has found some interesting reading.

What? This is the most intense part of the practice, I am hardly holding myself up, and now the instructor wants to opt out of counting and read to us instead?

Surprisingly, though, once she begins reading I get distracted from barely holding the pose, and it is actually easy to listen.

What if religion was each other?
If our practice was our life?

If prayer was our words?
What if the Temple was the Earth?
If forests were our church?
If holy water — the rivers, lakes and oceans?
What if meditation was our relationships?
If wisdom was self-knowledge?
If love was the center of our being?

As I write the poem here now, it almost seems like just words. In fact, after writing it I have to re-read it in an effort to get it.

It sounds nice, hopeful, and important. On the third read, I get that it's about interconnectedness, being connected to each other, to ourselves and even to the earth. I think it's even about the knowledge that everything we need already exists in and around us, and that it's all readily accessible.

But when I am in Wheel at the most intense point in both the pose and the practice, sweating like there is no tomorrow, I can hear the meaning without needing a high count in the reading. I don't even have to concentrate to get the profound message of the words. It all makes sense right away.

At the end of class, I roll up my mat and prepare to leave. I am almost outside the door when I decide to turn around to ask for the poem's title and the author's name.

I re-enter the studio only to realize that I actually already remember both. It is a reading of a poem by Ganga White called *What If?* I am surprised to even remember some of the poem's lines.

No need to ask. I had heard it.

The backbends had opened me up. Again.

Moon

Dancing in the moonlight; everybody feeling warm and right. It's such a fine and natural sight; everybody's dancing in the moonlight.

~DANCING IN THE MOONLIGHT, KING HARVEST

In many cultures, the moon is tied to motherhood.

It is a constant, always there even if it can't be seen. The pull of the moon is strong, rocking the ocean's tides in a timeless lullaby. Its light illuminates the darkness, no matter its shape or size.

I am a mother, and I've got the moon in my chart. I've had two astrological readings, one by an Ayurvedic astrologer and one by a Kabbalistic astrologer. And both speak of the strong presence of the moon, residing in some place with some sort of explanation, most of which comes down to the fact that mothering is big for me, and it's prominently in the house!

For many years, I've joked with my children about what I call the *Long Arm of Mommy*. It reaches through all the space and time in which they've grown, all the way to the independent young man and woman each is.

It's the part of me that's in them. It's how they connect to me without having lived at home during college and the years following. They both live on their own and make their own decisions; yet we are all still connected, so much so that when one calls, I sometimes answer with the phrase, *Get outta my head!* because we are so often in each other's.

Is it any wonder I've felt the pull of the moon all my life? That texts often fly around the family when the moon is full?

See the moon? reads many a text from one city to the other. *Look up!*

The other night at yoga, the instructor spoke of the moon and tied it to what he calls the Divine Mother. He said it's the brightness that's in all of us; that we all carry the light of the moon simply by virtue of being ourselves. It's automatically inside, even though it's ever changing.

Last night the moon was full, he announced. *Today, we are one day past, and already the moon looks different. There's a bit of darkness in the corner.*

Sometimes I've felt this darkness. There's a pull toward it when I'm not feeling strong. So I go to yoga to build my strength, to keep myself feeling bolstered, doing my best to make some muscles in my arms and my legs and my core, and also in my heart and my mind and my spirit.

This particular winter, for the first time in a long time, I had been dragging. My strength seemed to be waning as if I were the moon no longer full. Something was making me tired, and I wondered if it was the time change or the cold weather or the dark evenings.

Even so, I kept to my schedule, working and practicing, but the bed was calling this Divine Mother every chance it got. Before and after a practice, I'd catch a snooze. I lacked an appetite, and I had to be vigilant about getting in the calories. I literally felt as if I were fading.

I arrived at yoga one cold morning, bright and early. After practicing mostly at night, the early practice seemed doubly early. There, I pulled back my hair and looked up in the mirror. I could see only my face and my shoulders, and who I saw looking back seemed suddenly so small. I was never big, but with my hair away from my face, I appeared to me so frail; the muscles in my shoulders seemed to have disappeared in a moment's time.

I stepped away from the mirror and into the studio, feeling frantically far from whatever mothering light was supposed to be shining inside. It was very hot yoga, and I realized I had barely eaten the night before and had found it too early to eat that morning. I was on my mat, all too aware of my low reserves, depleted before I had even begun.

That morning I was the one in need of the long arm of a mother!

I finished the practice, doing two stints in Child's pose, unusual for me, and one errand to the front desk for a sugar shot of flavored coconut water, also unusual for me.

I got myself home, showered, dressed and started down the stairs to leave for the rest of the day but, halfway down, my tired bones told me to U-turn, and I listened. Hair and makeup done, I never made it out of the house, intending on a 20-minute nap but instead waking up with my face in the pillow two-and-a-half hours later.

The next day, I was back out and about, practicing again and trying to eat everything I could. I was trying my best to fortify what I had seen as that frail reflection.

And it was the day after that when I landed in the class with the instructor talking about the moon and about the mother in each of us.

We never stopped moving for an hour and 15 minutes with instructions to lift this and that, to reach here and there, first in one direction and then in the other. We were asked to add a little something of our own to each movement and then, surprisingly, told to toss aside our mats.

I think the instructor wanted us to flow freely with no boundaries in order to tap into the Mother inside, that strong and ever present brightness that's there regardless of how tired we are or how we look in the mirror with our hair pinned back.

When we finished, we came down to the floor, many seated moons of all shapes and sizes, illuminating the room with hands to forehead center.

Remember, the instructor said, *the light that is the Mother. She is you!*

With his words still echoing, I got myself home and looked to the mirror again. Miraculously, the muscles in my shoulders had seemingly reappeared in a moment's time.

And that night, I slept better than I had in forever, having finally been tucked in by the long arm that was my very own.

Strength

Put a little love in your heart. And the world will be a better place.

~PUT A LITTLE LOVE IN YOUR HEART, DOLLY PARTON

How long does it take to strengthen a heart?

I think that depends on what kind of shape it's in and whether it is a strong one in the first place.

The heart is a powerful, muscular organ that never rests. It beats continuously throughout a lifetime, and so it's important to provide it with the necessary nourishment, especially if it's a big one.

I've been trying to strengthen my heart.

It's a long overdue effort, but apparently my strategy to date hasn't been the most effective. I've basically preserved mine rather than fortified it, and it can't get stronger without the proper nutrients.

Yoga has worked on my body, and for the first time I've got some muscles going on. I could feel them especially in the beginning, when I first started practicing. I remember the aches as every muscle took note of the poses, and even now my muscles can still hold the memory of a practice, reminding me afterward of how hard they have worked.

These days, I feel strong and I am strong, and I make it a point to practice as often as I can so that I can get even stronger.

And I think it's affecting my heart.

For the first time in a long time, I can feel some aches there, too, as if my heart has been working as hard as the rest of me.

The other day, at yoga, we moved through the practice in an unusual way. Instead of our regular vinyasas, we did rolling ones, otherwise known as Water

Wheels. We first prepared with a warmup, moving in slow motion from Down Dog into Plank, tilting our chins to our chests, doming our backs and rolling out our spines until we were fully extended. From there, we lifted our chins and brought our hearts forth before tucking again to bring our hearts under.

We alternated between these movements, warming up our bodies and warming up our hearts.

I liked practicing in this way, but I didn't think too much about it at the time. I just moved slowly and with care, concentrating more on keeping my arms straight as I rounded my spine in much the same action as Cow pose, and then arched it in much the same action as Cat pose.

And then came the Water Wheels, and I dipped my knees and finally bent my elbows as I lowered my chest and then my chin all the way to the ground before pulling into Up Dog and crouching back and through, my heart skimming the floor before making my way back into Down Dog.

Throughout this practice, we continued to dip our hearts, and I did so while unaware. I really just continued to concentrate on the rest of my body, listening to the instructions as to what to do with my legs and my arms and even my navel, pressing it in to tighten my core.

When we lifted our hearts in Kapyasana, or Low Runner's Lunge, I really just focused on opening my hip and pressing my hands up and over my head. And when we lifted our hearts in Skandasana, or Side Lunge, I really just focused on getting low and spreading out my arms. And when we lifted our hearts in Vasisthasana, or Side Plank, I really just focused on balancing on one foot and one hand while lifting my knee.

I didn't know that all along I was feeding my heart the nutrients it needed just by moving in this way.

In fact, I didn't even know my heart was in on the action until we repeated the rolling Planks and Water Wheels again at the end. This time around, I felt a rush of emotion each time my heart dipped low, and it caught me by surprise.

Practicing is my plan to strengthen my heart just like I do my muscles. And I think it's a good one, too, as I seem to be able to feel it more than I did before. And even if sometimes I'm caught by surprise, I think it still counts for a lot.

Home

If you are lost, you can always be found.

~HOME, PHILLIP PHILLIPS

There's no place like home, and home can be any place.

I've never ventured too far from home.

I grew up down the street from where I now live. I went to the local university, and my biggest move came after college when I left campus for what was then my ultimate destination, a downtown Mary-Tyler-Moore-studio apartment.

To this day, although I am hardly home, I remain a homebody.

Having a home base has always grounded me, even though its location has changed half a dozen times.

And now, at this point in my life, I'm surprised to find another home at yet another location, this one being my yoga mat. No matter the day, no matter the weather, no matter the worry, I unroll my mat, and it's like coming home. I am secure and centered just sitting there.

Although I am no longer married, I remember well the time when I discovered this man would be my husband. We traveled out of town (a very big deal for me as I had never really traveled) and sitting there with him on the plane, I realized I felt at home, that it didn't matter where I was because home was now with him.

Then I was a single mom, making my home with my children, and we were good at it, too. I bought a house, settled us in, and there we spent their growing-up years, miraculously across the street from their grandparents.

My son played frequent catch with his grandfather, his Zaide; we'd spend hours sprawled on their couch watching television; and their grandmother, their Bubbie, joined us often at the kitchen table for afterschool snacks.

Always, just 62 steps away by my son's count, was another refrigerator with home-cooked meals and staples like ice cream, cookies, pickles, olives and more.

Now my children are many more steps away, living out of town and on their own, and my folks have moved not too far away, but away, as well. My siblings have been out of town for a long, long time.

And I have found yoga.

Yoga has brought me home in a way that is hard to explain, especially for someone who never realized she was far away in the first place.

How can I come home if I never left?

One of the studios I frequent was previously a townhome. There is a narrow staircase that leads to the first level, and the front desk even has a dishwasher. They serve tea and cookies, there's a sitting room, and the practice room has a fireplace and windows with curtains.

I am fairly new there.

The other night, the instructor called for our starting position, Samasthiti, or Mountain pose. We stood at the tops of our mats, one half of the room facing the other. This is the time to set our intention before the flow, and I looked around even though I was supposed to have my eyes closed.

It struck me that night as I scanned the now familiar faces that I finally felt at home there. I got that same grounded, home-based feeling as I rooted down through my feet and reached up to start the practice.

And that practice proved to be one of my strongest to date. I think it was because that secure feeling fostered a sense of confidence, and this confidence radiated in my body. I lifted in and out of seated straddle with an arm balance on both sides, my handstands were working well, and I was able to keep my legs up and straight in several Boat poses.

Mostly, I felt a core strength that literally lifted me through the practice.

Usually, I carry a sense of home regardless of where I am, and I think my children do, too. For them I think it fosters that same sense of security and confidence which, in turn, provides them with their own launching pad of sorts.

But still for me there is a deeper sense of home, one that seems age old. It is inside of me, and I think I lost touch with it for a while. This is the part that is hard to explain. This is the part that I found again in yoga.

There is something about the flow and the movement and the mat. It's the actual physical endeavor that seems to fortify my very core, the home base inside of me that *is* me.

This same studio had a meditation workshop where we all sat in a circle. It was led by a rabbi who provided instruction on brief, four-minute meditations.

On the first go, we closed our eyes. After a minute or two, mine sort of welled up and, as in Samasthiti, I quickly looked around, even though I was supposed to have my eyes closed. Thankfully, the rest of the room was doing a better job than I, and so my tears stayed private.

Afterward, each person was asked to explain the experience. Everyone had lots to say, but when it came my turn, all I could do was ask a simple question.

Why did it make me cry?

The rabbi didn't skip a beat. He responded with a simple but meaningful answer before moving to the next person.

In Hebrew, he said, *there is something called 'Teshuvah'. It means 'Coming Home'.*

Chicken Little

You can run, but you cannot hide. This is widely known.

~SHOWER THE PEOPLE, JAMES TAYLOR

When I was little, the mean girl in the neighborhood just terrorized us.

I was five or six years old and hung with my sister, older by a year. I felt safe with her. This girl would sometimes join the other kids from the block when we played outside in the backyard.

One day the mean girl pointed to the sky. We looked up and saw an airplane's leftover white trail cutting the sky in two.

The sky is falling! she hollered. *The sky is falling!*

My sister ran, and I followed fast on her heels, convinced the white line had sliced the sky from the air. We yanked open the screen door to the kitchen and let it slam behind us, considering ourselves safe on the inside while we peered fearfully outside.

I am afraid to say that I have sort of relived this scenario as an adult.

Once upon a time, I thrived on change. Change was exciting, and my 20's were filled with new changes almost every year. Graduation. A job. A marriage. A home. A dog. A baby. Another home. Another baby! One more home and a growing business. Life was dynamic, and we sailed along on winds that blew in all directions.

Somewhere along the way, though, I no longer welcomed change. My 30's brought a divorce. Big change! Three more moves, but this time on my own. More changes.

Raising my children, I encouraged accomplishments, tended accidents, changed schools and signed them up for all sorts of arts and sports. I fostered growth and change in my children, always. As for me, I took cover. I hunkered down.

And it was yoga that brought me back out.

When I first started yoga, many of the poses felt silly. It felt weird, and I was self-conscious, especially with the mirrors reflecting my body positioned in all sorts of newfangled ways. But in the studio there was really no place to hide.

We were instructed in Warrior I, a commanding pose in which the arms shoot up alongside the ears with one leg forward and one leg back, feet planted on the mat. It is a difficult pose if you feel powerful and an even more difficult one if you don't.

Warrior II was a little better, with arms spread out, front to back, and legs in a more comfortable lunge with hips to the side. And there was Yoga Squat that wasn't exactly so ladylike. And Down Dog, where we put our hands and feet on the ground and raised our hips, sometimes lifting one leg and circling it around.

We were expected to invert our bodies and stand on our heads. And my toes were always going the wrong way. I found myself always pointing them, a yoga no-no.

Thank goodness for the music and the easygoing instruction. It helped take me out of my head and into my body, out of stuck mode and into something brand new.

Over a period of months, my body changed. And my mind changed, too. I was lighter both physically and mentally, and I began to crave more. More in my yoga practice and more in my life.

One day at work, I attended an advisory board meeting. I was the note taker. Who knew my conscientious student days would pay off this way? I can take notes just like I could in college, and the result is practically a transcript.

At the end of the meeting, those on the board provided their thoughts on the subject matter at hand, the impact on the host company of the economic landscape in the coming years.

One by one, the board members spoke up, and I typed. I filled many pages before one of the last comments made me stop.

Just because the world is changing, the board member stated, *doesn't mean the sky is falling.*

I quickly pulled out a piece of scrap paper and wrote this down. His profound statement brought me immediately back to that little girl behind the screen door.

In many respects, I had raced behind that door again, thinking I was in a safe place when, really, I was just in a stuck place.

Stepping into the yoga studio has been like stepping back outside, bravely looking up at the sky and seeing that it is still in one piece after all.

<u>Truth 15</u>

Spirituality can be expanded
when faith is rejuvenated.

Space and Time

Baby, I've been here before. I know this room. I have walked this floor.

--HALLELUJAH, JEFF BUCKLEY

There's a song about a time for every purpose under heaven. *A time to be born, a time to die, a time to plant and a time to reap.*

Turn! Turn! Turn! is the refrain of this song that goes by the same title and gets its words from the bible.

But does time really turn over? Or is that just how we experience it?

My yoga practice is pretty athletic. It does not involve any deep thought about time or space, but afterward it seems to put my mind in exactly that place.

For me the practice makes a space where I can access some kind of spark that I think has been inside since the day I was born, and that has perhaps been in all of us since the beginning of time.

Some people think of this spark as the Divine, as the Light, as the energy source that is God. Whatever it is, I think I've discovered that I can access it through yoga. I find the ignition of this spark to be bright and brief. So to find it again, I have to keep going back to the mat.

This might sound oh-so-philosophical, but it's something I experience at a very basic level.

I come home from yoga, have something to eat, put my clothes in the wash and draw a bath. I climb in and sit there and all I feel is gratitude. The water is warm and so is my heart. I have even said some blessings aloud in the tub, and in this space and time they include those with whom I've shared love and those with whom I've shared hurt. In these expansive moments that follow my practice, I can see all the lessons that have come my way.

It's my belief that we all carry this inner spark. And if we expand enough to access it, the big picture that is our lives becomes illuminated, and our stories can start to make sense.

My yoga practice has led to a lot of reading about Kabbalah, the study of Jewish mysticism. Kabbalah explains that this lifetime is one of many that our souls experience, and it teaches that before we are born we reside with the Spark itself in a place where there is no space and time. And it's there where we can see the picture that is our lives, like a jigsaw puzzle with all the pieces fitted neatly together.

Kabbalah teaches that it's the choice of our souls to make their journeys back to Earth. And it's here where the new chapters of our lives are written, as we put together the pieces of our puzzles by correcting things within ourselves.

Such are our soul corrections, and such is the purpose of our lives.

These journeys of our souls and the concept of reincarnation are part of the ancient teachings of many religions, all of which have led me to reconsider the concept of time. Perhaps it's not as linear as I once thought. Perhaps it's not that every season turns; rather, it's we who return to every season.

I once took a yoga class that was choreographed in the round. We set up our mats in a circle and moved in circles ourselves. No one faced front, and we never left our mats but instead journeyed around and around, returning again and again to where we had started.

It was disconcerting to practice this way, but I was surprised that by the end of class I felt somehow restored. Something about it put matters right, as if I had gotten a chance to return and correct without fully realizing it.

So maybe our lives are like that practice, and we've been around on this journey before, putting matters right while traveling alongside some of the people we now know.

This concept is covered in a touching performance of *A Song For You* by three famous musicians and friends, Leon Russell, Willie Nelson and Ray Charles. Willie is crying as he knows Ray is dying, moved by the lyrics, *I love you in a place where there's no space or time.*

We are lucky if we have felt such love in this lifetime. If we have, then we've gotten a glimpse of that lit-up gift that is the Spark, and we've experienced something seemingly eternal, even if it's not lasting.

And it's not only love that lets us find this place where there is no space or time. I seem to be there when I practice and when I paint and when I write. It's where I move and the colors flow and the words appear.

I finish a practice or a painting or a post, and I wonder, *Where did the time go? How did I do that?*

And right away I know that I've been to another place, and that it was just a momentary visit. And what's been created can't possibly be replicated, because I am back in real time, the place where my lessons are learned.

When I want a break from real time, I unfold my mat. Most often it works, and I'm gone until I sit up from Savasana, or final resting pose. I sit there afterward feeling as if the past 75 minutes were only five.

When I question the instructor about the disappearance of time in the class, he explains that it happens because I've been traveling. He says I've been traveling on my breath.

Your day is based on the clock, and so time passes by hours and minutes, he says. *But your practice is based on the breath, and so time passes by inhales and exhales.*

I am grateful for this explanation, and it helps me understand why we try to lengthen our breath in the practice. Because why wouldn't we? Breathing is the way back to the Spark. It's how we are graced with snippets of this timeless space, the place where our blessings reside.

Crown

I'm picking up good vibrations. Good, good, good, good vibrations.

~GOOD VIBRATIONS, BEACH BOYS

Something's going on in my head!

I have to admit that what I like best about yoga is the workout. Each and every time, though, I am surprised by the aftereffects.

There is something spiritual about each practice. No matter the studio, no matter the instructor, no matter the style.

I'm not always conscious of how the practice touches my spirit; instead, I just know that I feel different afterward. After the practice, a kind of unconscious enlightenment happens. Gratitude rains down, and I feel expansive. It's as if each practice stretches my spirit another inch.

I am not very tall. I never have been. And ever since I was little, or I should say younger, as I've always been little, I've been patted on the head. To this day, as an adult, I still actually get patted on the head.

Turns out, the head is where our seventh chakra is located. It's called the Crown Chakra, and it's tied to our spirituality.

Several times I've been sitting on my yoga mat, waiting for class to start, and I get a pat on the head from the instructor passing by. Or I can be sitting at my desk at work and get a pat on my head from someone saying good morning. Even my grown children pat me on the head. I don't know how I never outgrew this, and at this point I guess I'm just kind of used to it.

It's just that before yoga, I never knew about the Crown Chakra. And, even though my crown has gotten lots of attention all my life, I am only now just discovering it.

I have to say that anytime there is good news or a coincidence when unlikely things *line up*, or I feel like I've just heard or witnessed something profound, I get goosebumps. But, these days, along with those goosebumps comes a feeling in my head. It's at the top on the left side, and it feels like a vibration or a tingling. Sometimes, not always, I feel this at the end of yoga when we sit with our hands in prayer, letting the effects of the practice settle in. The left side of the top of my head tingles.

Now, ordinarily, I wouldn't really ever go around talking about the top left side of my head vibrating. It sounds hokey, but I made a deal with myself to be honest when writing about my experiences in yoga, and this is one of them.

I think what I'm feeling is the energy in my Crown Chakra.

For many young girls a crown is pretty special, and growing up I was no exception. Every year I was a princess at Halloween. I didn't care about the costume or the mask. I only cared about the crown. I was a princess for the crown. I don't remember much from nursery school, but I do remember laying on my mat for naptime, trying to look like the best napper so that I could be tapped as the Sabbath Queen. I wanted to be chosen because the queen wore a paper crown.

I didn't know that all along I had a built-in crown already there, connecting me to something greater than myself.

Yoga has put me back in touch with my spirituality. It has made me re-evaluate my beliefs and how I fit in with the big picture that is supposed to be my life. I had no idea that moving around on a mat could do this to me.

When my children were in nursery school, as parents we joined them every Friday for something called *Shabbat Sing* and, really, that's one of the last times I was in touch with my spirituality.

Those Fridays would touch my spirits just like the yoga practice does now. I'd sit with my children in my lap, singing the songs I had sung as a child, feeling connected to them, to my younger self and to something even deeper.

The most important part of those Fridays was the visit from the rabbi. A kind and gentle man forever remembered, he would walk around the circle to bless each child. Patiently, slowly, and singing along, he would lay his hand on each child's head, giving his blessing to each in this way.

Maybe it is sacrilege to compare, but I think anticipating the approach of the rabbi and his blessings on their heads was probably akin to waiting for Christmas and meeting Santa. It was monumental for my children, the highlight of their week.

With his hands on their heads, the rabbi would acknowledge their spirituality, and they'd sit there beaming.

I just never knew then that what he was doing was igniting the energy in their Crown Chakras, and I didn't know that it would be another 20 years before yoga would do the same for me.

Religion

Divine teacher, beloved friend, I bow to you, again and again.

~ONG NAMO, SNATAM KAUR

I grew up in a fairly observant household.

My grandfather was from Poland, and my father was raised in an orthodox Jewish home. There were strict rules on the Sabbath. No driving, no work, no writing, no telephone. And the men and women sat separately in the synagogue.

But my father was a bit of a rebel in his younger years regarding religion and its related rules. As a child, on the day he broke his wrist my father was supposed to be sitting safely in Hebrew school, and not falling out of a cherry tree where he had chosen to sit instead. And as a teenager he was supposed to be walking to Friday night services, and not driving with a friend past the rabbi on the way to someplace else. He made a deal with the rabbi not to tell his parents.

He made no such deal with another rabbi a few years later when he snuck out of the *Yeshiva* to date that rabbi's daughter. Nor did this kosher boy tell anyone about his dates in Chinatown where he feasted on forbidden foods.

As a result, when I grew up, our household was less observant than that of my grandfather's and more in line with my father's comfort level. Even so, my father gave us a strong background in our Jewish heritage.

In my young adult years, I moved away from any religious observances but returned to them again while raising my children. At that time, the synagogue was a central and grounding part of our lives. But as my children grew older, our rabbi passed away, and I really left what connection I had with my religion. My sense of grounding from the synagogue was uprooted.

And now, after having been out of touch for so many years, I'm surprised to find that yoga has returned to me a sense of spirituality, something for which I wasn't really searching but am so glad to have found.

At the end of each practice, we sit with our hands in prayer. And sometimes the instructor talks about downloading some energy into the space opened by our practice. I breathe in and imagine inhaling some sort of positive goodness, which, by the way, I often see as the color white.

Sometimes he talks about letting go of something onto which we are holding, and I exhale what I imagine as some sort of staleness, which, by the way, I often see as the color gray.

And sometimes he talks about sending someone else some energy, and I imagine a whiteness falling like stars on the person about whom I'm thinking.

Some people believe that God is in all of us, and if that is so, then I figure that sending these falling stars, or my energy, is like saying a prayer.

Yoga has tapped into the spiritual side of me that had been slumbering for quite some time. That's not to say, though, that I haven't been connected to my heritage. I have, and there are several reminders throughout my home.

One is the painting in my kitchen from Israel of the Hebrew word, *Shalom*, or peace, along with a prayer for the home. Another is the pair of my great-grandmother's Sabbath candlesticks that sit on my dining room table. They traveled to me through the generations after being smuggled out of Russia in the middle of the night at the bottom of a hay wagon during the *pogroms*. And each room in my house is blessed with a *mezuzah* which holds a prayer from the Torah.

But truly it's been yoga that has made me feel part of something larger than myself, which I guess is what religion is really supposed to do. And somehow that is what has found its way back into my heart and into my home.

And so in the spirit of my spiritual growth, in addition to the *mezuzahs*, the Hebrew painting and my precious Sabbath candlesticks, I now have a little buddha that rests on the chest in the front hall.

He is smiling, facing the door to greet me every time I make my way home.

Blessings

I say a little prayer for you. Forever, and ever, you'll stay in my heart.

~I SAY A LITTLE PRAYER, ARETHA FRANKLIN

I have a buddha in a bubble!

My children surprised me with a snow globe that houses a golden buddha, seated in a peaceful womb of gold and glittering with sparkles that alight on his shoulders, his head, his hands, his lap and his feet.

Every morning, I shake my buddha! And I watch as my vanity lights illuminate the sparkles as they glisten and swirl in a dance to start the day.

At the closing of one of my very first yoga practices, I sat for the first time with my hands in prayer while the instructor said a few words. He instructed us to exhale what we no longer needed and to inhale some goodness in its place. After the practice, I was so hypnotized, I would have followed any instruction, and this seemed easy enough. I was surprised at how visual it was for me, and I exhaled what I imagined as the color gray, and I inhaled what I imagined as the color white.

During subsequent practices, he'd ask us to send some positive energy to someone we loved. At that point, I hadn't heard too much about energy, but I'd find myself visualizing this, too, and I'd imagine white stars falling on the person to whom I'd choose to send some love.

With some more years of practice under my belt, these stars have turned from white to gold. Somehow, now, for me, imagining these falling golden stars has become a sort of visual prayer, the kind I say after moving on my mat.

More recently, one of our instructors was not well, and for several practices during his recuperation, I'd find myself imagining him seated like a buddha with gold stars falling all around, landing on his head and sticking to his shoulders like ornaments on a tree.

And so it was with surprise that I received this most thoughtful of gifts, my buddha in a bubble, complete with sparkles as gold as the stars that I send in my prayers and sitting there like someone who's been blessed.

Every morning I look at this buddha, and I see the gold dust all over him. He's even sitting in some. And to me he looks blessed, and I see in this image that it's possible to be surrounded in blessings whether we know it or not.

Sometimes, for many, it can be hard to grasp such blessings, especially those that can't be seen or touched. But the blessings are there, because we are here.

On what I thought was just another summer day, the actor and comedian, Robin Williams, died. So did the daughter of a friend of mine who herself had passed away years earlier. And it made me wish that it could have been possible for them to have been sustained by the golden prayers that I'm sure were sent to them, and that I've no doubt they had sent to others.

For I'm thinking that they, too, were sitting in some gold dust, maybe even with some of it resting on their shoulders and in their hair and on their feet. And it's a safe bet they've even left some behind in their footprints.

I think it can be very difficult to exhale that which no longer serves us. Sometimes it can get stuck inside, and I think this may have been some of what happened to these souls. And it makes me wish that more of us would have known of their struggles, so that many golden prayers could have been sent to help in whatever way they might have.

The other night at the end of practice, a siren blared as we sat there in prayer with the room quiet and the sky dark. And the instructor said that, growing up, he was taught to say a prayer when a siren went by. And so he asked us all to do the same, to say a prayer for someone we didn't know but for whom, if we did, we'd love and bless, all the same.

I got home later that night and prepared to settle down for the evening, my buddha on the vanity, serenely protected in his globe. I picked him up and gave him a good shake. And as I looked inside, I saw that the vanity lights had formed a halo around his head, and I watched one more time as the golden blessings swirled all around and then settled down for the evening, too.

After, I took a picture to capture all that the buddha had in the bubble. And then I sent it to my children to say goodnight and share these golden blessings.

Reconnection

I've been searching for something taken out of my soul, something I'd never lose, something somebody stole.

~RIVER OF DREAMS, BILLY JOEL

You are loved by a God that is as close as your breath.

These words were hanging from the ceiling of a class I attended. They had nothing to do with the class. They were just part of the room in which it was held.

The class took place at night, a few hours after work. I had already decided to stay home and had changed into my evening get-up, a funny, striped, long tee with a half-sweater overtop and hockey socks on my feet. It's the outfit no one sees me in, but in which I am most comfortable.

For whatever reason, soon after, I changed my mind and my get-up, and got up to leave the house. I arrived at class, sat down and looked up.

Each word was written on a card and hung from a string across the ceiling. The first word, *You,* was missing, and the cards were not aligned. They zigzagged, and it was difficult to decipher. Throughout the class, I kept looking up, trying to line up the words. Before the evening's end, I had it.

You are loved by a God that is as close as your breath.

I have not really been breathing in yoga. At least not like I should. Even when the instructor reminds us to take more breaths, I don't always do it.

Breathing is supposed to be a big part of the practice. It's what makes the flow a moving meditation. If I am concentrating on my breath, I can easily leave my mind and connect to my body.

But some days find me feeling disconnected, as if something took my breath away. If you met me from the outside, you would think all things were connected. But I live on the inside, and I know when I am feeling a little lost.

When I found yoga, it seemed like a door opened to a new place into which I was invited. A bit skeptical at first, I put one foot inside. Then I started to feel the effects of the physical practice, and I eagerly jumped in. I embraced everything. The practice. My fellow yogis. A new diet. My mat. Even some new yoga get-ups, so much more attractive than my evening one!

I was part of a community, my spirituality awakened, and I felt connected to something greater than myself. I thought I had found some kind of answer in yoga, and I had not even known I had any sort of question. I just know that, for quite some time, it lifted and settled me simultaneously.

But now it's been a while, and I sometimes find one foot out the door. I don't feel so connected all the time, to the community or to any sort of greater good.

So now I have been searching again for a solution to a question which I'm not sure I can even posit. I keep thinking something is missing in my practice, but I think it is more that something is missing in me.

Perhaps it's true that whatever we carry on the inside comes along for whatever ride we take on the outside. And when it's time to breathe, what's on the inside can make an easy escape through the exhale.

When I came across those words hanging from the ceiling, it clicked. Might there already be some kind of goodness, even greatness, inside all of us? And might it be that our breath serves as a regular and secure reminder of this?

If this is so, then it would mean that nothing is missing, that none of us is ever really disconnected or ever even somewhat lost.

It was hot the other night at yoga. It was crowded. There was barely enough room to breathe.

There is a reason your mats are so close together, the instructor announced. *There is a reason it's so hot in here.*

Tell me why! I wanted to shout, but he was already explaining.

It's because everything you need is already inside you. That's where the joy and peace is.

Ah! It's like he had seen the cards, too.

The answer can be as simple as a breath. We have to breathe.

And with each inhale comes the reminder of something inside that's been there all along. And with each exhale comes the assurance that we are never really alone.

Energy

It's taken me a long time to figure out what yoga's all about, and I still don't think I'm totally there yet.

Really, at the beginning, I just dipped in for some exercise. I had no way of knowing that the practice would connect me, especially since I didn't even know I was disconnected.

Some people refer to yoga as a moving meditation, and I sort of discovered this without even realizing what was happening. I would just reach the end of the practice with some new kind of energy. All the while, I was not actually aware that I even stored any kind of energy, much less that the practice could shift it.

At the end of each practice, we sit with our hands in prayer. Sometimes the instructor takes us from the bottoms of our seats to the tops of our heads, talking about energy, talking about breathing into energy centers, talking about inhaling and exhaling and downloading positive energy.

In the past, I'd just follow along, supposedly using my breath to move some energy through my body and not really giving it too much deep thought. But that was then and this is now. Now, I am awake; whereas, before, I think I was sort of asleep. Somehow, moving on my mat has been like an alarm clock, jolting me from one state of consciousness to another.

This might sound like I've dipped in for some Kool-Aid along with the yoga, but practicing has introduced me to more of who I am, to my own energy and to that of others, as well.

Before, my perspective was more of *I am here, you are there, and sometimes we are here together*. But now I see that none of us is separate, even if we wish to be, because we are all made up of the same energy, the different levels of which impact our days, our moods, and ultimately, each other.

I am never over here while you are over there. We are always in the same place.

How else to explain the instant connections we feel with certain people, the automatic aversions we might feel toward others, the lift of our spirits when we see or think of someone we love?

It's the ebb and flow of energy that marks our experiences. Sometimes I can't put my finger on why it's a good day or a bad day, or why there might be a shift in my feelings or in that of another's. But now I know that this is energy at play, and it's more telling than any words I myself or someone else might say.

Meditation is supposed to help tap into our energy, and the moving meditation of yoga seems to do this for me. The practice creates a shift inside, and I move from a singular space to one that's intertwined with those around me.

I am still a beginner at meditation, and I've even attended a few workshops with a rabbi who has opened a mindfulness center. He has identified a tie to yoga, meditation and the ancient teachings of Judaism as a way to ignite his energy, and he is teaching others how to do the same.

Recently we sat in a circle, and the rabbi talked a lot about the breath, a big deal in yoga and in meditation. He said it's what ties us to God, or to what he calls the Source.

The Energy Source. The Light.

I was surprised to have stumbled upon this same idea by way of yoga. After the workshop, I mentioned an article I had written about a recent realization that the breath ties us to some kind of greatness inside, so we are never really alone, especially if we just breathe.

You knew, this rabbi told me. *The Torah is inside you.* And then he just looked at me as if to say, *Right?*

And it was as if he had blessed me with those words and the look that followed. I felt heartened because he validated a budding knowledge brought on by yoga, a knowing that I am connected on the inside as well as on the outside.

What he was telling me was that the Torah, or the Source or the Light, was one and the same as the energy that was *me*, and the energy that is all of us.

It seems that yoga has brought me back to myself. I think I might have been missing for a while. But if what this rabbi says is true, and I think it is, then I was never really gone.

My energy was just taking a rest, and yoga woke it up.

Acknowledgements

More than 20 years ago, I bought a writing desk. Over the years, it has served as a piece of décor, a place for framed photos, a mantle for Mother's Day cards and even a spot for old knitting needles. And I don't even knit.

For many, there are things we know without even knowing, and I think buying this desk had to do with something I knew! Somehow, I made this purchase for when I would write rather than if I would write. At the time, though, I didn't know it had arrived too early, before I had lived enough to learn and learned enough to write.

With that said, I am so grateful for the life I have, for the living I've done, and for the things I know without knowing.

Thank you to my children, Alexandra and Benjamin, for their love and support. To my gorgeous girl, Alexandra, a.k.a. Mary, whose courage and bravery set examples from which I learn every day. And to Ben, my beautiful boy, whose consistent strength and character make me so tremendously proud.

Thank you to my mother, Ruth Modlin, who was the first to listen to my words and has patiently done so ever since I was old enough to speak. I appreciate her wisdom and the confidence she inspires in me. As my editor, she is the stamp of approval for almost every article, and she provides the much needed push when I hesitate to express myself. Thank you to my father, Hank Modlin, too, for his love for my mother and for my children and me. And many thanks to my sister, Marla Lewis, who has been ever present for as long as I can remember.

I also want to thank my uncle, Joe Horenstein, for asking me to print and send my essays by mail. Compiling them is how I discovered I had a book, and his feedback encouraged me to pursue its production.

I am grateful for the opportunity to write which came to me through my practice when a local editor asked me to blog on all things yoga. One thing led to another, and now I'm also thankful for the welcoming venue provided by the editors of www.elephantjournal.com.

Thank you, also, to the Institute for Integrative Nutrition® and its online book course. The enthusiasm and encouragement of its leaders and fellow classmates carried me through the writing and publishing process from start to finish.

Finally, thank you to my yoga instructors and fellow yogis. There is a saying about how the teacher appears when the student is ready, and my practice has proved this true. Apparently, I remain ready, because I continue to learn. And I'm especially thankful for that.

CPSIA information can be obtained
at www.ICGtesting.com
Printed in the USA
LVOW12s1510040117

519724LV00006B/970/P